LEGACIES:

Stories from the Second World War

Compiled and Edited

by

Tom Swope

Radio Stew Press

radiostew@juno.com

Cleveland, Ohio

SECOND EDITION

ISBN-13: 978-1461012399
ISBN-10: 1461012392

Dedication

To my father.

And to Noreen and Michael.

Special thanks to

Uncle Bernie, Bruce and Don.

And to all the men and women who have shared their stories with me.

Contents

Preface

The history of the Second World War has been well documented in historical archives, but war is more than facts and figures. Each battle is a collection of unique moments experienced by individual soldiers. We have read the accounts of the GIs that hit the beach on D-Day, but what were the twists of fate and the life choices and the coincidences that put those soldiers in that place at that time? A life during wartime is a personal journey and everyone has a story to tell. Ask veterans about their experiences and they will tell stories of friendship and fear, of sadness and hope. Maybe they'll remember a brush with death or a moment of faith. Or maybe their most vivid memory of the war is the day the latrine blew up and all they could do was laugh. These are the stories you rarely find in official accounts.

In October of 2000, Congress authorized the creation of The Veterans History Project. The purpose of this Library of Congress project is to collect and preserve firsthand accounts of wartime experiences for future generations. A few months after the project was announced, I volunteered my services. Since early 2001, I have recorded stories from more than 400 World War Two veterans and those who served on the home front.

I work in radio and, after just a couple of interview sessions for this project, I was convinced these personal stories would make a compelling series of radio programs. LEGACIES: *Stories from the Second World War* features highlights from some of the oral histories I have recorded. On each show, guests talk about their lives from the day their war began till the day they finally came home. LEGACIES premiered on the Fourth of July in 2001 and is currently broadcast on a Cleveland area radio station. LEGACIES has won two Ohio Excellence in Journalism Awards and was named 'Best Weekly Radio Show in Northeast Ohio' at the March of Dimes A.I.R. Awards.

I have been overwhelmed by the support I have received from the local community for my work with veterans. The radio show has attracted a loyal following and I am proud that I have been able to do my part in presenting these stories and bringing these men and women the recognition and respect they deserve.

Over the years, I have had numerous requests for print versions of the stories heard on the air. My goal was to create a forum for veterans to share their memories in their own words and I believed the radio show served that purpose. But not everyone has access to the radio programs and that is why I have compiled this collection. Many of the stories you will read were originally broadcast on LEGACIES, but this book also includes written material I have not used on the program and photos I have received since I began my work on this project.

As the narrator for the LEGACIES radio series, I always limit my comments. I want to give the guests as much time as possible to tell their stories in the time I am allotted. I try to help move the story along, but my intent is for you to hear (and read) the words of the men and women who lived through this historic time.

More often than not, the recording sessions for these stories took place at the kitchen table and I always hoped to make it more of a conversation than an interview. I rarely knew the veterans before we talked, but we quickly developed a personal connection. These new friends were telling me about one of the most important times in their lives and they appreciated the fact that someone was willing to take the time to listen. Many told stories they had never told before. I have corrected some grammatical errors, but not all. For the most part, these are the unedited words of the men and women who were there.

LEGACIES: *Stories from the Second World War* is not a complete history of the war. These are just a few of the millions of stories lived by ordinary people during an extraordinary time.

...we here highly resolve that these dead shall not have died in vain...

REMEMBER DEC. 7th!

Some of the men we were carrying to the common grave were not yet dead. They were in a coma. We were told to bury them. As bad as things were and as low as our morale was, and as abandoned as we felt, we knew that someday the United States Graves Registration Service would be through here for those bodies and provide those men with a decent burial.

Richard E. Francies
U.S. Army

Richard Francies enlisted in the Army in 1937. He joined the Army Signal Corps and specialized in the operation and maintenance of radios. When he completed his training in the States, he had to choose an overseas assignment. The other side of the world sounded good to him.

My 1ˢᵗ sergeant and I didn't get along too well. He was an old-timer and I was a young kid. I was in New Jersey – Fort Monmouth, New Jersey – and I said, "How far away from here can I get?"

He said, "Oh, Philippines. We got a good post in the Philippines."

"Fine, put me in for a transfer to the Philippines." That was in about November of '39 – I guess it was. Within several months, I was in the Philippines.

At the time, the Philippines had a reputation as being a great place to serve.

The Philippines was 'The Pearl of the Orient' and it was the playground for the Army. It was nice. It was real good. There were lots of bars, lots of places to go visit, and ah, lots of girls. It was real good duty. 'The Playground of the Pacific.'

On December 8, 1941, Richard had about a week to go before he would be leaving the Philippines and heading for home. But he was rousted out of bed early that Monday morning. The radio room was getting reports from Hawaii – reports about an air raid on Pearl Harbor.

I went up to the radio station and got behind one of the operators and watched him copy what was going on in Hawaii. The reports were coming from Fort Shafter. They said, "The planes are flying over." Then there would be silence for a while and then he would come back on and he said, "They just dropped some bombs around here."

I said, "Oh, no."

The attack on Pearl Harbor was part of a coordinated assault on various targets in the Pacific. It was obvious the Japanese would soon be attacking Manila. Richard's outfit moved their operations out of the city.

We stayed on the outskirts of Manila for a week or so. I installed some mobile units in the trucks and we provided radio communications for the convoys going back into Bataan.

Eventually, the 228th was also moved to the Bataan Peninsula. The Americans and their Filipino allies held out for four months against an overwhelming force of Japanese attackers.

April 8th (1942) came along. They had just called the radio truck back in and I was in the signal depot – repairing equipment and things like that. That's where all of us ended up, in the mountains just above Mariveles. During the night, there was a lot of noise outside and our officers went out to see what it was and there was one of our French seventy-five (millimeter) *guns. They had moved a group of them back and they were roughly where we were and one of our officers said, "You belong at the front line."*

They replied, "This is the front line right now."

"Oh." And the next morning it came down to, we were surrendering.

The men had only two days of rations left. They had no choice but to surrender.

Our officers told us to walk down to Mariveles. It was probably five miles or something like that. They said, "You're roughly on your own now because we don't know what's going to happen." So, a number of us started to walk down the road to Mariveles – down the zigzag trail. We finally got down to the bottom and they said to fall in with larger groups. Being in a real small group of a half dozen fellas, you just might get shot. We fell in with a larger group down there and the Japs came down and just surrounded us there and told us to put all our arms down. But when we left the signal depot, we had our rifles and our 45s and we disabled them. We took them apart and threw the pieces in the jungle, so we didn't have any (weapons).

The men were ordered to wait in an open field under the hot sun.

The Japs left us sitting there for three days – no food, no water. Then, they started to move us out in groups of a thousand and we started back up that zigzag trail, right up past the signal depot where we'd been.

The Bataan Death March had begun.

Then we just started on the march. There were a lot of artesian wells along that road and we'd go through the different villages and some of the fellas – when they were out of water – would break out of line and run for the wells and the Japs would shoot them, just for going and getting water. Well, finally we decided if five hundred of us go for water, somebody's going to get it. So that's what we did. A whole bunch of us would go for water and at least some of us got water. The Japs just didn't shoot randomly. What they did was put a big ring around us and, with their bayonets, force us back on the road.

And as for food, they kept saying, 'Food next town. Food next town.' Well, there was never any food when we reached the next town.

Along the way, Filipino civilians tried to help the prisoners.

Women and children were standing alongside the road looking for their husbands, their sons, their friends. And they saw the shape we were in. We were in pretty bad shape. So they started throwing us food wrapped up in banana leaves and the Japs would go over and beat the women and sometimes shoot them or bayonet them, just for throwing us food. And they even killed – I didn't see any of it – but they even killed some of the babies the women were carrying.

As the march dragged on, the POWs grew weak from starvation and they were vulnerable to deadly jungle diseases.

I got malaria and I felt an attack coming on and I was getting dizzy and I knew I had to step out of line. I had to get someplace where I could sit down. I was real reluctant to do it because when you fell out of line or you fell and couldn't get up, your friends weren't allowed to carry you and the Japs would either shoot you or bayonet you. So I had to be awfully careful. As we were rounding a curve, I saw a fence. There was a lot of shrubbery growing up and there was a little opening in there. I looked around and didn't see the guards in either direction and I slipped through that opening and got inside and sat down on a log. I was dizzy and just a disaster. All of a sudden, I felt a tap on my shoulder and I looked up and here was this Filipino man. I said something to him, but he didn't speak English. He was a real elderly man. I made a sign with my hand like a mosquito came and landed on my arm and bit it to show him I got malaria. He understood that. He said to stay right there and he would be back in five minutes. He came back with a Jap corpsman. I thought 'oh boy, now what am I going to do?' The corpsman didn't speak English, either. I did the same thing to show him I had malaria and he nodded his head and he pulled out a hypodermic needle and put some medicine in it. He could have been putting acid in it, I didn't know. He handed it to me. He wanted me to give myself the shot. I said, "Uh-uh. You." So he gave me the shot. After that, he stood there for five or ten minutes and I started feeling much better. He motioned for me to get back in line. I motioned for him to write a note because if I just walked back out there – Bang! And he understood. He wrote a little note and he went back out to the line with me. Sure enough, one of the Japanese guards saw me and came running up. I handed him this note. He looked at it and he jabbered something to the corpsman and they chatted for a second. Then the guard just went on his way and the corpsman went on his way and I went back in line.

The men marched nearly seventy miles.

The whole march for our group of a thousand lasted eleven days. We got up to San Fernando, near the train depot, and we just sat on the ground. They made us just stay there for a few days until a train came. When the train did come, they pushed us into boxcars. Then they slammed the doors shut. It was a thirty-five-mile train ride to Capas. We were packed so tightly in there that if somebody died – they would die standing up because when they let us out, there were always bodies in the cars.

The prisoners got off the train at Capas and were marched to Camp O'Donnell.

And I don't remember that walk at all. All I remember is getting out of that boxcar and we just started walking. The first thing I remember is when we got to Camp O'Donnell, the Japanese camp commander gave us a welcome speech saying, "You are my prisoners and you will be treated as such."

Hundreds of prisoners died at Camp O' Donnell in the short time that Richard was there.

After three or four weeks, they called for a communications detail and the officers picked out fifteen of us. The Japs took us down to Manila in trucks. They had taken over Fort McKinley, which was on the outskirts of Manila. All of the barracks were intact and they had put all of our captured radio and telephone equipment in one of the barracks. They moved us into that barracks. The Japs were in all the other barracks all around the post. They showed us all of the equipment and then they said, "Fix it!" They wanted to use it.

Richard took advantage of his job and fixed up a radio so he could get a little news from home.

While we were repairing the radio equipment, I'd have a receiver upside down on the bench – testing equipment and reading a meter – with earphones on, listening to KGEI, San Francisco. We had all the news reports. The Jap who was in charge of us was an elderly man. He wasn't military. He was more like Civil Service. One day, he came over and tapped one of us on the shoulder and said, "San Francisco no good. Tokyo, okay." So we fixed up a receiver for him to listen to Tokyo. And he was happy. Then, we still listened to KGEI. So we had our news from the States and we were aware of what was going on, as long as the detail existed.

The men made an interesting discovery about their neighbors at Fort McKinley.

Right next to the barracks that we were in, there was a smaller building and some Filipinos set up something like a PX for the Japs. And the Japs would go in there and get their tea and cookies and things like that. After a while, we were allowed to go in there. It was run by four Filipinos and we never said much to them. Finally, when we started talking, we found out they were actually four guerrillas, running the PX. They said they knew what we were doing – fixing radio equipment – and they said they needed radio parts.

Francies and the others found a way to smuggle parts to the guerrillas.

They had these little passenger carts pulled by horses and they always had a basket hanging underneath for the horse's food. Underneath the basket went our radio parts. We kept that up for quite a while.

If the POWs were caught doing anything like this, they would be executed.

If they'd have known of the things that we were doing, they could have used us for pincushions for their bayonets time and time and time and time again. We were sabotaging the equipment. We were smuggling parts to the guerrillas.

One day, Richard thought he had appendicitis. He went on sick call and, in the doctor's waiting room, he had an unusual encounter with a Japanese soldier.

And I sat down and waited to be called. Two Japs came in and sat down beside me and after a little while, I looked at this one fella on my left. I asked, "Do you speak English?"

"Yeah."

"Where'd you learn English?"

"Well, I went to the University of Southern California."

And finally I asked him – I didn't know if I should or not, but he'd been in the States – I said, "You know how this is going to end up, don't you?"

And very dejectedly he said, "Yes, I know."

After about a year on the communications detail, Francies was sent back to a prison camp. Several months later – in 1944 – the Americans were closing in on the Philippines and the Japanese decided to move many of the able-bodied POWs to their homeland. The ships that took the prisoners to Japan were known as 'Hell Ships.'

It was a pretty rough trip. There wasn't a whole lot of food. We did get some water every day. A couple of times we were allowed up on the deck and they sprayed us with salt water and we got some fresh air.

For toilet facilities on the Hell Ship, they had a great big wooden bucket in the center of the hold we were in. Every once in a while, they would lift it up and dump it overboard. That was the toilet.

They arrived in Japan in September of 1944. The prisoners were to be used as slave laborers.

And we were going to a copper mine – a Mitsubishi copper mine – up at Hanawa, Japan. They took us up to these new barracks they had made. It was a nice building and everything. Cold, though – no heat. In the wintertime, it wasn't like the snow we get here. It was measured in feet. They had furnaces – little pot-bellied stoves in each one of the barracks. We would steal anything that would burn and bring it back and build a fire. Sometimes, when the Japs found out about it, they would come over and put the fire out.

When the Japanese were finally convinced they could not win the war, an order was issued about what should be done with the prisoners.

(Reading from the Japanese order)

"2. The Method

(a) Whether they are destroyed individually or in groups, however it is done, with mass bombing, poisonous smoke, poisons, drowning, decapitation, or what, dispose of them as the situation dictates.

(b) In any case, it is to not allow the escape of a single one, to annihilate them all, and not to leave any traces."

Richard later learned that the POWs in his camp were to be executed on August

29, 1945. Fortunately, on August 14th – several days after the second atomic bomb was dropped – the Japanese accepted surrender terms.

The Japanese commander told us that the war was over and he knew we were going to want more food and this and that. And one of the things our officers asked for first was some cans of yellow paint and paintbrushes because we knew that someday the observation planes would be flying over. They sent some of the fellows up on a roof with the yellow paint and the paintbrushes and they painted: 'Hanawa, 550 POWs.'

Sure enough, one day not too long after that, an observation plane did fly over. We didn't see it. We just heard it. The next day, Navy torpedo planes came back and circled the camp and dropped a message saying: 'When the observation planes flew over, they took pictures. They developed them and saw writing on the buildings and they enlarged it. We came back to investigate. You're in an unmarked prison camp and we can't drop you any supplies now, but we have already radioed Saipan and your supplies will be up tomorrow.' And the next day, B-29s did come up. We had never seen a plane that big. The biggest plane we ever saw was the B-17 at Clark Field. They dropped us food and clothes and medicine and everything.

Fifty-seven out of every one hundred prisoners taken in the Philippines died in captivity. Like many survivors, Richard Francies asks the question:

Yeah, why am I alive? That has bothered me for a long time. Why am I still alive?

Perhaps he survived to tell his story.

Circumstances are as they are, but I can choose my attitude towards them.

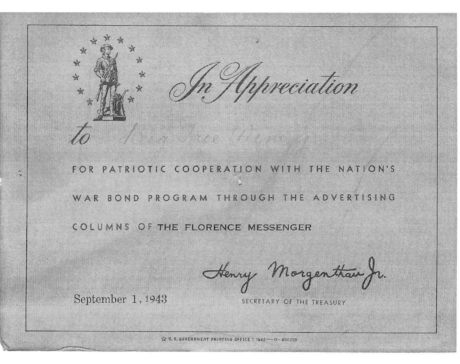

Pitching in on the home front

I remember sitting in front of a little table model Atwater-Kent. My mother was there with me and I remember yelling, "Good!" when they announced that we had been attacked and we had declared war on Japan. And I remember my mother being quite shocked. She looked at me and said, "Don't say that. Don't say good. It's not good." But I was glad that we were finally in the war and were going to help out.

Aaron S. Fox
USMC

When Aaron Fox was a senior in high school, he decided to enlist in the Marines.

I had to fake my mother's signature and I told my principal at Glenville High School that I was going to be leaving. I still had the 12-A to complete. He was very shocked. I was a fairly good student and he said, "Well, all you really need to do to get your diploma is complete a course in trigonometry. Take your trig book with you and if you're able to, study, and then we'll send you an exam and if you pass it, we'll send a diploma to you." So, that was my high school ending.

Aaron kept his word and took that book with him to boot camp.

I had the book and when boot camp was over, it came time to be assigned to different advance training things – infantry, etc. One of the officers saw the trig book and he said, "Did you study that?"

I said, "Yeah."

He said, "Well, we'll make you a forward observer." I didn't know what that meant, but I became a forward observer for artillery. And you have to do a little bit of geometry in your head to figure out the elevations and so on and so forth. And that's how I became a forward observer.

After six weeks of advance training, Fox shipped overseas to a staging area in the Pacific. He joined the 3rd Marine Division, 12th Regiment, 3rd Battalion. On July 21, 1944, they invaded the island of Guam.

Going over the side of a troop ship on what is known as a Jacob's ladder is a very harrowing experience. It's just a rope ladder, you know. You've got your rifle and your pack and then somebody above you stepping on your fingers as you work your way down. The Higgins Boat, the landing craft, is bobbing up and down in the swell alongside the ship, like a cork, and it's a very small-looking thing as you go down this ladder. When you are ready to let go of the ladder and jump into that boat, you'd better time it just right or you're apt to fall between the Higgins Boat and the ship. And that

13

happened. Many guys slipped. There were accidents.

You jump into the Higgins Boat. You're jam-packed in there. You really can't see over the gunnels. And you're roaring towards shore and suddenly you grind up on the sand and the ramp drops and the guy yells, "Get Out!" The coxswain of the landing craft wants to back that thing out of there and leave as quickly as he can, so he wants the Marines off. So off we went into the sand and scurried around until the officers got us organized and we started proceeding inland into the jungle.

Aaron was eighteen when he landed on Guam. At first, it seemed like a great adventure.

It's not that you didn't have any fear. You think that nothing can happen to you or your mother will raise Hell, you know. It's strange, but I did not have any fear at that moment, at that point in time. So I scurried back and I was excited. I mean it was like watching a movie. It was almost like an out of body experience, if you will. I mean, I was watching this young guy thinking 'Hey! You joined the Marines and here you are in a battle.' Just like – what was it I saw just before I enlisted? <u>Guadalcanal Diary</u>. I remember seeing that thing and saying, 'Wow, I'd like to become one of those guys.' So suddenly I was one of those guys.

After that, the excitement wore off and the misery of trying to survive in that jungle took over. It was hot on Guam. Mosquito-ridden. Malaria-ridden. Muddy. You were never dry. And the mosquitoes never stopped biting. We came down with a variation of malaria called dengue fever and when guys came down with that they were just wracked with bone-breaking pain.

The campaign to take Guam lasted about a month.

We got the high ground. There was no organized resistance, etc., and Guam was quote, 'secured' – that's the Marine term for it – in thirty-one days. But that's a myth. That's a fallacy. We were competing with the division on Saipan for who could secure their island faster. But then we settled into areas and the real war began. We would have patrol activity daily. We'd send platoons out into the jungle chasing down these stragglers and there were thousands of them that just drifted back into the jungle. And that was very hard duty...very hard duty that went on day in and day out for months and months and months.

In February of 1945, Fox's outfit was told about their next mission.

We got the word that we were going on a campaign. Most everybody assumed that it was Iwo Jima because we kept hearing broadcasts that the Navy planes were bombing this little island. And when we got aboard ship, on deck, the officers briefed us. They had a map of this little island that was shaped like a pork chop, two miles by four miles. And they said there's this volcano – an extinct volcano, Suribachi – at this end. And they told us that it was Iwo Jima and that the Navy had been bombing it for 102 straight days. Hopefully, the resistance would be neutralized, but don't count on it.

February 19, 1945 – the invasion of Iwo Jima.

And this was a little bit more intimidating than Guam had been. I remember going over the side, going down that Jacob's ladder – trying to spot that Higgins Boat bobbing up and down. Jumping as the Higgins Boat came up, luckily. And we were all in there, very quiet, and there was a lot of water and oil sloshing around the bottom of the boat. And there was this guy that we called 'Pappy' because he was all of thirty-two years old. He was kind of a portly guy and he was rather tense. He used to call me 'Foxman' and he said, "Hey, Foxman, do me a favor." He said, "The strap on my legging is loose and I don't want to trip." He says, "And I can't bend over."

I carried a weapon that is known as a B.A.R. – Browning Automatic Rifle. How I was saddled with that I don't know, but the thing weighed more than I did. I weighed 145 pounds in those days and the ammunition belt and that weapon weighed more than I did. But at any rate, I gave him the weapon to hold and I knelt down in that cold, oily water and fastened his bootstrap for him and he was very grateful. He thanked me. He never – he never saw his thirty-third birthday. He was killed. And we sustained, as you may know, very, very heavy casualties on Iwo Jima. But you know, some live and some die and you can't figure out why and how.

Nothing could prepare the Marines for what they would face on Iwo Jima.

When we disembarked, immediately the Japanese on Mount Suribachi had mortars, small five-inch field pieces, heavy machine guns, all zeroed in on the beaches. Each division had a different section of the beach and we were all assigned different movements. The 5th Division was to go up the beach, straight north. The 4th Division was to go across the island, which was two miles, and then go up the other beach. And the 3rd Division – mine – was just to go inland a little bit and then go up the center. Well, the best laid plans, etc., etc.

It became chaotic because when we hit that beach it was deep, black volcanic sand. It was like being on the surface of the moon, literally. There was no vegetation. And guys just couldn't move. We got bogged down. The tanks, trucks, our half-tracks, got bogged down and they were there every which way, at different angles, just askew. And casualties. Bodies all over. Screams for corpsmen – Navy corpsmen – those were the medics. "Corpsman! Corpsman!" A lot of screaming. Lot of chaos. Lot of smoke. Lot of smell. And this was a nightmare. This was a nightmare.

The beach-masters were the men with the bullhorns who were assigned the job of getting some order on the beach and they were bellowing orders do this and do that. One of the orders was, "Pull those bodies out of the way!" – so that we could lay metal mats down to get these vehicles ashore. And so it was like stacking cordwood. Just throwing the bodies out of the way; it was as if they were not human. Soon the vehicles were able to get some traction and to move over this first ridge where the ground was somewhat firmer and they could move. It was inch by inch that first day.

On February 23, 1945, there was a moment that lifted the spirits of all who were there: the raising of the flag on Mount Suribachi.

I was not far. It was very visible from where we were. When that flag went up, there were literally hundreds of ships off the beach there and everybody hit their horn, you know. It was just an experience that's hard to explain, but everybody froze where they were and you could feel the goose bumps, you know.

The flag raising boosted morale, but the fight for Iwo Jima was far from over.

I was assigned to the 21st Marines as an observer and I would travel with their skirmish line. My job was to call fire from the guns to support this skirmish line and make sure that our shells were landing where they should.

To get coordinates and information back to the artillery batteries, the F. O. teams used a unique code.

In my forward observer team, there was a lieutenant and an NCO, me, and in each group we had Navajos, code-talkers. We would string wire and call back information and if it needed to be coded, the Navajos would do it in their language and the Japanese that might be listening in couldn't understand that.

After nearly three weeks on the line, Fox finally got a break from combat.

I was up there with the 21st for about eighteen days. Then they gave me a break. They pulled us off and said okay, you're going to get a couple days of rest. And their idea of rest was to put us on a burial detail. Marine bodies were pulled back and put into covers. The Japanese bodies were laying there in the sun and they were rotting and there was fear of pestilence.

It is hard to imagine any job worse than working on a burial detail.

One Japanese had died on his hands and knees with his head buried in the sand, his hips elevated, and his tunic had slid down his back. And the sun was beating down on the middle of his back and it raised a huge blister. And to one of the guys that was with me – and I refer to him as an idiot now – I said, "Don't touch that." But he grabbed this corpse by the back of the tunic and pulled him over backwards and that blister broke and a smell emanated from that thing that I cannot to this day describe. But we had to handle that corpse and get it in the ground. For days afterwards, I kept washing my hands, trying to get that smell off. Well, the smell wasn't on my hands. It was in my nose, in the olfactory nerves or cells of my nose, and it stayed there for days and I couldn't eat anything because of that smell. It was like anything I was eating was dead flesh. But that was our rest. The burial detail.

After his 'rest,' Aaron went back into action.

When we went back up on the line, I think it was March 8th (1945), *the biggest artillery barrage in the history of the Marine Corps took place because we were coming to the final concentration of Japanese strength at the northern end of the island. The commander of the island had his bunker there and we just tried our best to blow everything apart.*

The Marines had utilized and thought they perfected something called a 'rolling barrage' where we would drop a line of shells maybe a hundred yards at the most in front of an advancing skirmish line of infantry. And the trick was to keep raising the elevation so that the shells kept dropping in front so that there would be a wall of artillery explosions. Sometimes, shells could drop short for various reasons. The powder might be wet. Instead of seven bags of powder being loaded, six would be used in the excitement. It didn't happen often, but when it did and the shells fell short on our guys, the artillery was referred to as 'Murder Incorporated.' The Marines had a black humor – always.

Well, I called fire for that thing and finally the infantry got to the very northern end of the island. There were sheer cliffs there – and a lot of Japanese civilians, who had been living on Iwo Jima, chose to jump over those cliffs to the rocks below rather than surrender. There weren't many, but some Japanese soldiers did surrender at that point. They came out of their caves.

Some of the Marines scaled down that cliff, got to the ocean, filled some five-gallon gasoline cans with water and sent them to the commanding general saying, 'Water from the northern end of the island. We're here. We secured the island. But this is not for consumption.'

Fox left Iwo Jima on March 20, 1945.

I got back to Guam and immediately started training again and found out that we were going to be the spearhead division for the invasion of Kyushu, the southernmost island of Japan. And so we were training with specific tactics, which would have been, of course, futile. And we did that until one day a guy came running through the tent area yelling, "Hey, they dropped a magic bomb! The war is over!"

"What?" We figured he was drunk on the native drink – fermented coconut juice that we used to drink called 'Tuba' which was almost a poisonous beverage. But he was celebrating and they had dropped the bombs on Hiroshima and Nagasaki.

In early 1946, Aaron came home, and saw his best friend.

I had a dog since I was in elementary school and the dog went all through my schooling with me and survived the war. And the high point of my homecoming was to see how my dog, 'Blackie,' would react when he saw me. And the dog came up to me and smelled me and he was getting old and at first, he didn't realize it was me. But then, it dawned on him. He recognized the smell and the hair on his back just stood straight up and he started jumping hysterically. He wouldn't stop and everybody just wept at watching that dog.

Incidentally, Aaron Fox **did** graduate from high school.

I got my diploma on Guam. I didn't have to take the final exam in trigonometry. The principal wrote me a very nice letter saying that the school owed me a debt of gratitude and I sure deserved my diploma.

Well, they call it 'The Longest Day,' but it seemed pretty short. I know that one fella came over and he was all excited. He saw a leg laying all by itself on the beach. I said, "What's your problem?"

He says, "I never saw a leg blown off before."

"This is a German leg. Don't worry about it. The body's not going to bother you."

Some people could accept seeing this stuff and others couldn't. As an example, in 'Private Ryan' they showed basically what it was like and a lot of people can't stomach that. But that was what it is. War is not get shot in the shoulder and put your arm in a sling. It's lay there and bleed to death and scream and holler. You can take it or you can't. That's what I think caused most of the emotional problems. It never seemed to bother me. I don't know – a lack of feeling or whatever.

George T. Doyle
U.S. Army

George Doyle received his draft notice while he was still in high school.

My birthday was in May and I got a deferment to graduate. They deferred me for three months. Otherwise, I'd have been gone before I even graduated from high school. That's the rate they were taking them.

He was inducted into the Army in September of 1943. After basic training, George volunteered for the infantry and joined the 90th Division. He trained with the 90th for three months and then shipped out in March of 1944.

I was not seasick, but many of the men were. We had nothing to do but lay around on the ship and that type of thing. We couldn't do anything really and we just stayed either above or below deck. We all couldn't be in one place at one time because there were so many of us on the ship. That was the Affelone Castle that we went over on and I understand it was sunk by U-boats on the way back to the States.

The trip across the Atlantic took seventeen days.

We landed in northern England and our regiment went to Wales, just across the border from England – a thousand yards or something like that inside of Wales – and we trained there for a couple of months. The rest of the division was in England and we didn't know why, but then found out that the 1st and 3rd battalion of our regiment that was in Wales made the invasion while the rest of the division came in D plus two, three, four, whatever. So I was in combat two or three days before the division is credited with landing.

Doyle's outfit was to land in support of the 4th Division on Utah Beach on D-Day. George believes his training for the invasion of France left much to be desired.

Our invasion maneuvers consisted of full field pack, everything we owned, and we marched across a stream about eight feet wide – about six inches deep. That was our invasion maneuvers. I had yet to climb down a cargo net. I happened to be fortunate that when the LCVPs were filled, they filled the first one on deck and then lowered it over the side. When it comes back to pick up more men, they have to climb down a cargo net. Most of our guys never climbed a cargo net until they were shooting at us. But we read about all the well-trained troops. We were not well trained. We were poorly trained.

As D-Day neared, troops were secretly moved into position.

We moved from Wales down to England. We were on the coast in an area that was under heavy camouflage and we had to stay in our tents all day. In the evening, we could go outside. We could go to the mess hall and they showed movies all day long, but you couldn't be observed outside. Where the camouflage was, you could go one way or the other and that was about it. And that was in artillery range of the French coast. Forget their airplanes. They could get us without any trouble with the artillery.

In late May of 1944, it was obvious the invasion was coming soon.

We stayed there for probably a week and then we went through town and we were loaded onto a boat – I can't remember the size or anything – and we went out to an LCI, Landing Craft Infantry, and we went aboard. We were an over-strength company, of course. There was two hundred or two hundred ten of us. We got on there and one of the sailors said, "You might as well take your stuff off."

"Well no, we're going back."

"No, you're not getting off till you get to France."

That's how I found out we were ready for the invasion.

The men waited for the word to go. And waited.

We were running out of rations and with the invasion being postponed, they thought we might have to go back to England to get food. Well, it ended up that they went on the 6th of June, instead of the 5th. I'd say I spent seven days out on the English Channel kind of going around in a circle in that weather.

They had five thousand or fifty-five hundred – depending on who you quote – boats out there. And that was a big job; getting all that coordinated. We didn't realize how big it was at the time. But I'll never forget coming across the channel and seeing all the boats, behind us or in front of us, with the barrage balloons on the front and the stern, so that strafing planes could not get down too low.

D-Day: H-Hour plus three.

Yeah, we pulled in and the Coast Guard pilot dropped the front end. That was the landing barge where the front end drops down. And the first guy, Andrew C. Nutt of

Fordyce, Arkansas, stepped off – and he was about six-two, six-three – and he went in over his head. I was standing next to him and I grabbed his equipment and pulled him back in. Then they pulled us in another hundred feet or so and when we got off, it was still chest high to me. Had I stepped off where we were, I'd have gone two feet under water with all that equipment. When you get that stuff soaked, you're pretty heavy. We did have life belts, but I didn't feel I wanted to be floating around out there. That's a bad place to float. You want to keep moving and no way with all the stuff you're carrying, could you have been able to swim. Everybody had to carry extra ammunition. Although you didn't use a mortar, you had to carry a mortar round, so that way there are a hundred guys and you had a hundred rounds of mortar ammunition on the beach. We carried wire, which would have been used for Headquarters Company, for the telephones and that type of thing. We had to carry that. Everybody came in carrying much more equipment than they would ever need themselves. My version is, we were expendable. They put men in there that had never seen combat and they saved the good troops for the follow-up. Makes sense, but you wonder whether you wanted to be in the better troops or not. They kind of figured that they would lose x-number of people the first day and therefore, better to get rid of the less-trained troops. Makes sense if you're not one of them.

George wasn't thinking of the glory of war when he hit the beach.

What was I thinking? I think it was just one foot in front of the other and trying to get in there without getting killed and not knowing what you're going into and you knew there's no way back and you couldn't turn around and go any place because the ocean was behind you. It's a long swim back to England. I don't know that I had any great thoughts, just get my behind up there and get out of fire.

It was a horrific scene.

But when I came ashore, there were bodies from the 4th Division floating in the water at that time and we had the easy beach.

They soon realized they had landed on Utah Beach in the wrong place.

And I think what helped us greatly was, we landed a mile and a half away from where we were supposed to. And the 4th Division commander, Barton – between he and (Brig. Gen.) *Roosevelt – decided okay, we'll start here instead of reloading and going back out and moving, which would have been a disaster, trying to climb up a cargo net.*

So, we started to fight from there and that changed everything that we had known about maps and all our landmarks were different. It was kind of a do-your-own-thing type of thing, which is a great advantage. In the German Army, if your officer didn't tell you what to do, you didn't do anything. We were much more on our own, for good or bad. But mostly I think it helped us a lot. The initiative of the American is a little different. Everybody is the boss.

For a few days, George's outfit was held in reserve for the 4th Division. On D plus four, they were sent into action for the first time.

During our first attack, one of the fellas got shot in the leg and he happened to be the lead man in the regiment. He took off running and if you know how artillery works, they fire five hundred yards ahead of you and keep increasing as you move forward. We weren't supposed to run. We just ran into our own artillery and our casualties the first week or so were from our own artillery. But this is what happens. You can't govern that. When you're scared or you're wounded or something like that and you take off on a dead run, there's no way for artillery to know that. Now, you have communications between everybody. We didn't have that.

The green troops of the 90th Division were ineffective during the early days of the campaign in Normandy.

We had very poor leadership. We didn't get anything done right for the first couple of weeks and they were talking about breaking up the division and using us as replacements, we were so inept. And then we got a commander and turned everything around and by the end of the war, Patton said we were one of his best infantry divisions.

About a week after D-Day, Doyle was wounded on Hill 122.

'122' means it's a hundred and twenty-two feet over sea level, and from the top of that hill you had a view of the entire beach. The Germans had the hill and we had to take it because they had observation and they would have been able to shell the boats that were unloading equipment, food, whatever, that we needed later. So, it ended up that we took the hill and consequently got surrounded. There was a lot of heavy fighting and I got hit ... where did I get hit then? I got hit in the back. I was facing forward and a shell landed behind me. I got hit in the back and actually, it wasn't too bad. The 1st sergeant patched me up and I never did leave the area. I got a Purple

Heart that day. I got the Combat Infantryman's Badge and I got my sergeant's stripes – in that area, that day.

George quickly became a seasoned combat veteran.

There was one time when we were dug in right next to a hedgerow that was about five feet high and one of the fellas said to me he thought there were Germans on the other side. I climbed up and looked and there were German tanks along the road within six feet of me. So I went back to the lieutenant and I told him, "Those are German tanks and there're troops sleeping on top of them, so we have to get out of here."

And he said, "No, those are our tanks."

*I said, "Lieutenant, I've been here too long. Those are German soldiers. Those are German tanks. I'm pulling my squad out. You can do as you please." He said he'd court-martial me. And I pulled my squad out and it ended up that the whole platoon followed, including the lieutenant, and they **were** German tanks. So, instead of court-martialing me, he gave me the Bronze Star.*

Later in the campaign, George received a second Bronze Star.

I had to go up to the pillbox we used for company headquarters. I had to go there for something and there was a lot of shelling going on and hand-to-hand combat very close. The lieutenant came in and asked if we had a mortar. I said yes and he said he needed mortar fire. So okay, tell me where. Well, he told me where and I couldn't get anybody else to man the gun so I had to set it myself and fire it. The range was so close, they were afraid to throw hand grenades. And I dropped the shells where he wanted them, practically straight up. If you're familiar with a mortar, you can fire it straight up in the air and it'll come straight down and, had the wind shifted, I could have blown myself up. He came back and said, you did a good job and everything, and I blew his ear off with one of my mortar shells. That's how close his men were to the enemy. So, he gave me a Bronze Star, too, because nobody else would go out and fire the mortar.

After the Normandy breakout, the 90th Division advanced across France and kept doing their job. There were no victory parades for these grunts.

I do remember one thing, though. We went down a road and we could see the Reims Cathedral straight ahead of us. We went off a road to the right and then made a left turn and we saw the Reims Cathedral from the side. We weren't allowed to go through Reims. Basically, that's what happened in Paris, too. Although we fought up to the outskirts of Paris, the French drove through and they and the 28th Division – with their nice, clean uniforms – marched through town. They didn't want us guys that needed a shave and smelled like heck to walk into Paris.

On January 5, 1945, George was wounded for the second time.

This is a case I shouldn't admit. I had 'stolen' – I should say – a Czechoslovakian 81 mortar and I got 81-millimeter mortar ammunition from a supply sergeant, and the platoon leader, my gunner and I went out with the mortar and we were just playing around, practicing. I had also borrowed a German range finder and wanted to figure how to use that. Well, we kind of made a mistake. We hit a truck convoy and they got mad and they fired back and I was facing forward and I got hit in the stomach. My gunner was facing the other way and he got hit in the back. And the lieutenant didn't get hit, but he almost got court-martialed because we were supposed to be in a holding position, not causing trouble. But this is the American ingenuity. You saw something. You shot at it.

After that second wound, Doyle was offered a furlough.

The second time I got wounded, I had been told I had a pass back to the United States. I'd have to work on a hospital ship and I would get two weeks at home and then come back. So I'd be off for about a month. But when I went to the division hospital, I got a letter from my company commander asking that I not leave the division because, if I left, I would go to a replacement depot and end up anyplace. So they patched me up there.

Instead of returning to the States, George went back to his unit. On his way to the front lines, he had an encounter with General Patton.

I was taken from the hospital and taken up to the St. Vith area and there was a sign there: 'St. Vith 6 Kilometers,' or something like that. There was a jeep sitting there and I recognized it as a general's car. It had the stars on it. And I think it was a major came over and asked me why I didn't have a helmet and why I didn't have a rifle. So I explained, they took me out of a hospital and sent me out there as is. He went back over and explained to General Patton. He waved and drove away.

On February 6, 1945, Doyle was wounded for the third and fourth times.

The third was just before the Prune River in Germany, after we had closed the gap on The Battle of the Bulge and moved forward. They let the lead company go down the road and our company was in reserve. Then as we came up to a certain point, they laid in artillery fire. They had the first unit trapped, so they hit us. And what I found out later was that thirteen of us got hit and the other twelve died. I got hit in the top of the head and that was my own fault, too. I got some new men in and I wanted to make sure that they were down and dug in and I stood up. I got hit, but they got killed. That was about six in the morning. It wasn't quite daylight. Then about six or seven o'clock that night, as it was getting dark, I rolled over to get my canteen and got hit again in the back of the head. And I just laid there until an artillery officer found me and took me back to division hospital, wherever it was. Then I was transported to Liege, Belgium and the doctor that operated on me in Liege and took some of the shell fragments out of my brain was from my hometown. He worked at Cleveland Hospital, which is now Metro. So, on the operating table, we discussed the city of Cleveland. Of course, I was in no pain at that time, but I was conscious.

With these wounds, George's war ended and he was sent home.

Subsequently, I went to Paris, then the London area to hospitals. I came back on the Queen Mary – four and a half days on that trip. I went to Halloran General Hospital on Long Island for one or two nights and then went to Martinsburg, West Virginia at Newton D. Baker General Hospital. I had a plate put in my head and I had it taken out and put back in. The total from the day I got hit till I got discharged was a year and ten days in the hospital. I still have a piece of shell fragment in the cerebellum and a plate in the top part of the skull missing in the back.

After Doyle got home, he tried to get in touch with some of his old Army buddies.

I wrote to three or four different people. I wrote to the fella that I pulled back out of the water. We were in basic training together and I knew him from there. He never wrote back. My gunner got hit the same time I got hit in January and I never heard from him again. I was close to my platoon sergeant and I wrote to his folks when I got home and I got a letter back, 'I'm glad you knew my son, etc.' I didn't know he was killed. I wrote to a woman whose husband was my platoon leader, a lieutenant out of West Point that was a very nice person. I got to know him in the two or three weeks he was there. I found out that he was killed the day that I got wounded. And I lost my stomach for writing to people. Those letters – they don't cheer you up when you first get home.

HELLRIEGEL'S VETERANS'
43rd PEARL HARBOR DAY
REMEMBRANCE

Monday, December 7, 2009

Silvio and Albert Welcome You!

HELLRIEGEL'S INN
The Inn with the
Country Club Atmosphere

Beginning in 1966, Hellriegel's Inn in northeast Ohio has presented an annual 'Remember Pearl Harbor' dinner on December 7th. The dinner began as a veterans-only event to honor Pearl Harbor survivors, but it is now open to all who wish to commemorate Pearl Harbor Day. After I began my work with World War Two veterans, I was invited to attend the dinners. The first year, I met a half dozen Pearl Harbor survivors and I interviewed them for the LEGACIES radio series. One of those I met was Norm Shure. He gave me this story of his memories of that day.

Herbert Norman Shure
U.S. Army

I was drafted into the Army on 7/3/41. After three months' basic training at Ft. Belvoir, 1500 of us were sent to Schofield Barracks, Oahu, Hawaii to reform the 34th Engineers Regiment in late September 1941. When Pearl Harbor was attacked, my company was on detached service, building Camp Ulupau, a new C.A. camp, at Kaneohe Bay Naval Air Station. The new camp under construction was located approximately midway between K.B.N.A.S. and the A.A.F.'s Bellows Field. Both facilities were demolished in two bombing raids. The first raid came from the north and perhaps a dozen dive-bombers struck and practically demolished K.B.N.A.S., then at treetop level, came south and strafed us and Bellows Field. The second raid came from the south, dive bombed Bellows, strafed us and K.B.N.A.S. We lost one man. Both facilities lost many more.

For many months after, I felt guilty because in the initial excitement I thought I might have started the whole war. I was eating breakfast with a good pal from Cleveland. We were having scrambled eggs and he handed me a new bottle of ketchup, which I never used on eggs. But he insisted, and after months of resisting his urgings, I tried it. Well, nothing came out. So I pounded on the upside-down bottom and a large glob exploded on my eggs. At that exact moment a huge building-shaking noise lifted the table, plate and all. Dishes fell off a wall rack in the nearby open kitchen and my friend, Mike, looked at me as though I had committed an unspeakable crime. I peeked into the open neck of the bottle, saw nothing but ketchup and handed Mike the despicable thing.

But everyone started running outside and at the open doors, someone shouted that K.B.N.A.S. was in flames. Mike and I ran out, saw huge billows of black smoke rising from underground fuel tanks and we both climbed onto the roof of the latrine behind the mess hall to get a clearer view of what was going on. Then the last plane to drop bombs came across strafing and I knew we were all in trouble when I saw and heard machine-gun bullets hitting the dry soil beside and below us and raising little clouds of dust. The plane, with a large red disc on its fuselage, was turning in a bank to align his plane with Bellows Field. We clearly saw the pilot looking at us. We rapidly climbed down to the urgent sound of a bugle calling everyone to assemble. And in my mind I kept thinking: Could I have started it all?

After the attack on Pearl Harbor, Norm Shure requested a transfer to the Army Air Force. He became a weatherman with the USAAF and was sent to a base in Prestwick, Scotland. There, he met a girl from Dumbarton, Scotland and they fell in love. Her name was Ishbel. After V-E Day, Norm returned to the States, but he stayed in touch with the girl from Scotland. A couple of years after the war, Ishbel joined Norm in America and they were married.

Ishbel belonged to a 'War Brides' association and, in 1982, she was asked to write about her most vivid memory of the War. Aside from meeting Norm, of course, this is what came to mind.

Ishbel Shure
'Enchanted Moment'

On Monday, May 5th, 1941, the Clydeside, in Scotland, was mercilessly 'blitzed' by the Luftwaffe. My Aunt was killed while driving her car as an auxiliary ambulance. Two of my cousins were injured by shrapnel from the same land mine that killed my Aunt. Our family had lost its immunity to death 'by enemy action' and my brother-in-law decided to get his womenfolk and children away from the shipyards, which were ostensibly, the targets of that bombing.

Next day we packed clothes and essentials and he drove us to Ardlui – a hamlet at the top of Loch Lomond. My brother-in-law had a petrol (gasoline) allowance because he was an amputee. After delivering us to our destination, he returned to Dumbarton to keep his cinema open and serve in his volunteer role of air raid warden.

There was a full moon that Tuesday evening – what we called a 'bombers' moon' – and as I walked along the banks of Loch Lomond listening to the cuckoos singing and drinking in the indescribable beauty of my surroundings, the war seemed far away and unreal.

We had managed to book two rooms in the hotel in Ardlui. My sister and her ten-month-old son shared one room and our mother and I and my sister's stepson, the other. I was sharing a double bed with my step-nephew who had a hacking cough which kept me awake. He was a very restless sleeper, thrashing around, flailing his arms. It was impossible for me to get to sleep.

Suddenly, out of the silence of the night, there came the throb-throb of the diesel engine German Heinkel bomber – a sound which had become familiar to all of us. The sound increased to a thunderous roar and I was certain that this was 'it' – the plane was going to crash into the building we were in. It was an indescribably terrifying feeling. At once, there was the loudest explosion I have ever heard in my life and everything shook and lo, there we all were, intact, listening to the plane climbing again.

There was a great hue and cry – people rushing out into the hallways in their nightclothes and curlers.... Some went outside to try to see what had happened. Some of the maids were thrown out of their beds. One had become deaf.

There was no sign of real damage – no crater and the hotel, the only large building around, still stood, so we all went back to bed to wait until morning, praying that was it for the night. I remember being so angry that the children were being subjected to this kind of terror as I fed a bottle to the baby to get him back to sleep.

The morning of Wednesday the 7th of May was a perfect spring morning. I walked down by the Loch amid the daffodils, primroses, bluebells and bog myrtle, all with their heady fragrances. It was so beautiful, it tore at my heart.

After breakfast I took the two small children for a walk along the road, the younger child in his stroller, the elder walking beside me with a hand on the stroller handle. We gathered some sphagnum moss to take home to use in making the dressings for wounded servicemen – something I worked on in the Burgh Hall in the evenings – and as we were walking, I saw a boy about my age (15) coming toward us on a bicycle. I met his eyes with mine and, in a strange moment of intuition, I knew what was going to happen next. He got off his bike, set it on the ground, came up to me and without saying a word, he smiled and kissed me. Then he picked up his bike, straddled it and rode off. It was one of those rare and beautiful moments in my life that I will never forget.

The children asked no questions and I didn't attempt any explanation. I felt the beauty of that day in May in that most beautiful of places combined with the fact that we had survived whatever terrible thing that had happened the night before had evoked in both of us a desire to celebrate just being alive! It was absolutely perfect and absolutely beautiful.

We later learned that a bomber had intended to drop a sea mine into the Holy Loch nearby where the British had submarines based – this Loch is salt and flows into the Atlantic Ocean. Having missed its target, the mine had struck the mountainside instead. The sound of the impact on the rock was magnified by the water all around. Other than the minimal blast damage and the tremendous noise, all else had been spared.

I cannot remember what the boy looked like – that isn't important. I sometimes wonder if he ever thinks of that enchanted moment as I do from time to time.

Courtesy of Leonard Solomon

When I went to Bremerton, we were given the opportunity to pick the ship we wanted. If we got it, we were then allowed to designate where we might want to work on the ship. And of course, I liked aviation so I picked the flight deck. Fortunately, I was given an opportunity to go aboard the Enterprise and I also went up to the flight deck, so that's where I started my naval career.

Stephen Puttera
U.S. Navy

Steve Puttera enlisted in the Navy in August of 1940. After training, he requested duty on an aircraft carrier. He joined the crew of the USS *Enterprise* as a boot seaman.

A 'boot'? He don't know nothing. He's a greenhorn. He's a brand new service person, so to speak.

Before the war began, the 'Big E' took part in training exercises and patrols. It was all fairly routine stuff, until the day Hollywood came on board the ship.

And I watched them do this. They made a movie that was called <u>Dive Bomber</u> and the scenes in that film were taken off the Enterprise and I saw all that. I enjoyed that. I had a chance to meet Errol Flynn and Ralph Bellamy and who else? There were a couple others there. And being that I was on the flight deck of course, I had a good chance to talk to them and I did. It was fun. It was enjoyable.

The *Enterprise* was the flagship for Admiral 'Bull' Halsey.

And in fact while I was still a seaman, I talked to Halsey, personally, on the flight deck. I happened to have the duty one day and the duty officer says, "The admiral wants a chair. You take a chair up to him." He was up on the flight deck looking out and I brought him the chair and he talked to me, just like you and I are talking. I was surprised. He says, "Son, what are your plans? How do you like the Navy?" Here he is worrying about a war coming, because we were close to it and he knew it, but he talked to me like that and it was very impressive.

In 1941, America was hoping for peace, but preparing for war with Japan. In early December, the 'Big E' delivered planes to Wake Island. The carrier was scheduled to return to Pearl Harbor on December 7th.

After we dropped the planes off – on our way back – it was then that we had orders to arm all of our aircraft and even our guns. We were ready. We were on 'Ready Alert' on the way back to Pearl and we were supposed to be in Pearl on December 7th and docked. In fact, the Japs had an 'X' marked where they figured we would be moored, but rough seas and refueling 'tin cans' – destroyers, we called them 'tin cans' – made us a day late. So call it what you will, we were a day late and so we missed it.

The Japanese had hoped to catch the entire Pacific Fleet in Pearl Harbor, but the aircraft carriers were out on assignments when the attack came.

In fact, we were about 150-60 miles out when the Japanese were hitting Pearl. And as was our custom, we had sent five or six planes in to arrange for a berth and it was only then that we realized or learned that Pearl was under attack because our pilots radioed back to our ship. Up until then, there was radio silence. They didn't tell us anything, so we had no idea that they were under attack. Maybe they didn't even have a chance to tell us because they were busy. So anyway, that's when we first found out.

Understandably, the defenders of the Hawaiian Islands were very nervous that day. Anti-aircraft gunners shot at anything in the sky.

Of course, there was a misfortune. The ground forces there at Pearl shot down three – that I know of – of our planes and maybe a fourth. But in the melee, one of our planes also shot down a Japanese airplane. That was our first encounter with the Japanese, although we on the ship didn't see any action. We were away from it. The only ones that saw it were the pilots in the SBDs that we had sent in.

When the crew on the *Enterprise* heard the pilots' radio reports about what was happening at Pearl Harbor, some just didn't believe it.

Betting – a lot of betting. Some of them were betting it was a drill and some were betting it was real. I had a hunch it was real and it was.

The reports were confirmed and they were ordered to search for the Japanese fleet.

Well, we were out hunting the Japanese and we didn't go in until nightfall. And of course, that's when I saw everything that had happened. They were lined up along the sides of the bank because we were not that far from the bank – maybe a couple hundred feet – and they were saying, 'Where were you? Where were you? Why weren't you here?' and all that. Well, we didn't know anything about it. They could have broken radio silence. Why they didn't, I don't know. They were under attack. They might as well have broken it. But we didn't know it until our pilots told us. At least, that's from where I stood, anyway, and I was on the flight deck and we were getting firsthand information.

Pearl Harbor was a heartbreaking scene.

Well, it's hard to describe. You don't want to believe what you're looking at, I guess.

But the sailors on the 'Big E' didn't have time to dwell on that.

They put us to work. We had to refuel and reload, re-arm, and go right back out. We were only in there a few hours. Come daybreak, we were back out to sea and then from then on, we were hunting subs, ships, whatever we could find. And of course that started our action against the different islands and the Marshalls and Gilberts were the first ones we hit. After we hit them, on our way back, they tried to get us; but we were lucky and that gave our gunners the first chance to fire at enemy aircraft. They did shoot down a couple, but we weren't hit. We were nearly hit. Bombs landed close, but not close enough to hurt anybody. We might have lost one man, I think, from shrapnel from a bomb that exploded close to the ship.

In April of 1942, the *Enterprise* was part of a top-secret mission. They led a task force that included the USS *Hornet* and sixteen B-25s under the command of Colonel Jimmy Doolittle. Their mission was to bomb Tokyo.

The Hornet wasn't that far away and I saw every plane take off, every one of them. The seas were rough. It was really rough and we weren't supposed to launch them then. But I also saw the ship that we sank that had spotted us. We didn't sink it. One of the destroyers, or was it a light cruiser, sank it. But then Admiral Halsey decided that instead of coming in to four hundred miles, we would launch the planes. We were about six hundred miles out and it was too far, but it's like the movie shows. That's what they apparently did. I wasn't on the Hornet, but I know what they did. They did take extra cans of gasoline and they took off. We watched them take off and we cheered when they took off because we knew where they were going. But we were the ones that provided the fighter escort and the search ships that went out, so that we wouldn't run into anything. We were the ones that escorted them. The Hornet gets a lot of credit and they did a good job, but all they did was ferry the planes out till they were launched. We were doing all the work. Not that we want the credit. It was just everyday work. We're not looking for no credit for that, but we took them out there. We were experienced and the Hornet wasn't.

Puttera was eventually promoted to flight deck director on the carrier.

I was a 'Yellow Shirt,' they were called. In fact, we were the ones that were in charge of landing, launching and re-spotting aircraft.

When the *Enterprise* went into action, they had some very long days.

We could have three or four airplanes in the air, or maybe we could have forty or fifty in the air. And the planes would land and the arresting gear hook would engage the arresting gear cable. And of course, one of the crew on the plane handler crew would unhook the wire and then we had plane directors all along the flight deck to bring the planes into the spots up forward. The flight deck was long enough to land all our planes. Some, we would send down one of the elevators, if they weren't covered up. We had three of those. One up forward, one amidships and one after. Once the planes were landed, they were then refueled, re-armed and re-spotted. In other words, re-spotting was put them back on the after end of the flight deck again, so they were ready to take off. And we always had them in perfect position. They were packed in there so close that the wing tips would maybe be four to six inches from the prop of the plane beside it or in front of it.

And with dozens of planes preparing for takeoff, everyone on the flight deck had to be extremely careful.

We had orders to have our helmets buckled. We just had cloth helmets then. On the SBDs, you had a pilot and a rear seat man, who was a radioman and a gunner. One day, this rear seat man apparently hadn't buckled his helmet and from what somebody saw, his helmet blew off and he instinctively reached for it, got his arm caught in a prop and it just made hamburger out of him, that's what it was. So, here I am, in charge of what's going on. We can't waste no time because we're hitting someplace – and I don't remember what we were hitting. And this didn't happen very often, but the pilot whose prop hit this kid was really shook up. He kept shaking his head 'no' when the plane director wanted him to move. He wasn't going to take off, so we had to pull him off to the side. It took maybe ten or fifteen seconds. It couldn't have been more than that. But to them up on the bridge, that's a lot of time and they're hollering on the bullhorn "What's going on? Get that plane off!" I hurried up and had the plane pulled off to the side and we continued the launch. Then they called me up and when I explained what had happened, I was commended for doing it so quickly.

After all the planes had been launched, the remains of the dead airman were removed.

But I do remember this poor kid. At the after end of the flight deck, there was a little rail that stood up and a lot of him was pushed up against there. I even picture in my mind – I won't forget it – some of the corpsmen with a bag or a basket shoveling him up and putting him in it. I remember those things.

In the heat of battle, there is a great deal of confusion. One night, a plane was cleared for landing…and it wasn't one of ours.

There was one engagement and I'm not sure if it was Midway or not, we almost landed a Jap airplane. It was at night and we were landing our planes and he was lost and I saw the red ball go right by the ship. I'm on the flight deck and I'm watching him go right by and he went in the drink somewhere, I guess.

When planes land, arresting cables are stretched across the deck of an aircraft carrier to catch hooks on the tails of the planes to slow them down. The cables usually work quite well, but Steve remembers a frightening accident.

The cable snapped and it whipped around like a rubber band. One end was attached and it broke loose on the starboard side and hit four guys. It scalped one, hit me in the shoulder, one guy got it in the knees and there was one other one. I don't remember if he was killed or not. But the guy that was scalped – his name was Osborne – I remember the name. He was at our reunion here a couple of years ago, so I talked to him. He was okay.

He was okay and obviously very lucky.

The cable had hit the top of his head and just took the top of his head and hair off. They pulled it back and sewed it so that you could see the scar, but he had some hair and everything. And it was not bad. But that's our way of talking. We didn't care. 'Scalped.' He was 'scalped.'

The USS *Enterprise* (CV-6) survived twenty major engagements and became the most decorated ship of World War Two.

All in all, we must have had some good luck because even with fifteen or sixteen bomb hits, they never sank us. One time, a bomb hit aft and that could have been Santa Cruz, but it knocked our steering out of commission and here we are going in a circle. If there had been a Jap around, a sub or any more Jap planes had come in, we were just going around in a circle – a half- or three-quarter-mile circle. We were doing that for maybe a half hour and I'm thinking, nobody better come around. We're helpless. When are we going to get straightened out? But I think it was the chief down below decks that somehow got it fixed and we were steering again. So he was the hero. He had to be decorated.

The 'Big E' lost many brave sailors during her tour of duty. Puttera recalls the eerie aftermath of a devastating bomb hit on a gun mount.

The guys were pitch-black from the bomb explosion. All the powder magazines that were there ready to be used had all blown up and were set afire. Most of the guys were already examined when I saw them and their mouths – this way and this way and this way and this way – were red. And I remember this is how they cut them so they could pull the lips open and check their teeth. And that's the only way they could tell who they were.

Steve Puttera served on the *Enterprise* for more than three years. That is a long time on a vast and lonely ocean. Every sailor who spends that much time at sea has a story that will make you wonder.

I slept in the starboard catapult. I slept there and the catapult operator slept there. I don't think we had anybody else. Me, being 1st class and the chief in charge of the flight deck, I could do what I wanted – sleep where I wanted. So I slept there. This is a funny story. But one particular night, I heard somebody out in the water calling my name. An agonizing voice: "Help me! Help me!" you know.

So I sat up in the bunk and I said, "Hey, wait a minute!" I said, "There's somebody out there calling my name. Somebody's overboard and they're calling me to help them."

"Oh, go to sleep. War nerves. War nerves. Go to sleep."

Puttera tried to put it out of his mind, but the voice sounded so real.

After one of the engagements, we got back to Pearl. It was maybe two or three months later. I got a letter from my mother and she said she got notice about a friend named Bob Buerth. Back home, we had a club called 'The El Gauchos.' Bob Buerth was one of 'The El Gauchos' and we were good buddies, real good buddies. This was before the war. So when I joined the Navy, he went and joined the Navy. Well, he was in a 'tin can' in the Atlantic. That's where they stationed him. They were dropping depth charges on a sub and somehow he was knocked overboard and never found. In the letter, she said the date when they said this happened. I thought back and it was exactly the time I heard that voice. It's funny. Funny thing. Exactly. It's a funny thing. So you wonder sometime. Is there something, some kind of telepathic thing that can go on? You know, we've got our guardian angels, I'm sure, and everything. So, I don't know.

In late 1944, Steve was injured on the flight deck.

We were bringing planes forward. This was about three o'clock in the morning and we were getting ready to attack someplace. And I'm walking along with the planes and one of the flight deck officers and all of a sudden, this fighter wing swings out and hits me and knocks me into the back of this flight deck officer. I busted my nose and the wing hit me in the back and broke the third lumbar vertebra in my back, which laid me on the flight deck. I was immobilized. I guess they wondered where I was, but they launched the aircraft. Eventually, I crawled to the island structure.

He spent about a month in sick bay.

And when I got back up on the flight deck and resumed operations, I got a letter. My dad was in the hospital. So I figured, well, I'm going to try to get off the ship.

Like all who served on the USS *Enterprise*, Steve Puttera is convinced she was the best ship in the Navy.

Nobody cared about themselves. That's one thing on our ship. Nobody ever cared about himself or didn't seem to. He thought of the other guy. There was camaraderie on that ship that was on no other ship that we ever knew of. A lot of it on a lot of ships, but I think we had the greatest. We really do think we had the greatest. That's why she stayed afloat, I think.

GENTLEMEN — THE
TARGET FOR TO-NITE-

You were in there and you were by yourself. You were closed in. There was a hatch door and the way you entered it from the inside, you would crank the ball so the guns were pointing straight down, open the hatch door and climb in. You close the door and then with the controls turn the ball and change your position so that your guns are parallel with the bottom of the airplane. Obviously, for a city kid from Massachusetts, sitting in that ball turret – hanging underneath there, and nothing between you and space except what you were in – it was quite an exciting experience.

Phillip C. Vincello
U.S. Army Air Force

When America entered World War Two, Phil Vincello was a student at Boston College. He decided to join the Army Air Force Reserve. They had a plan that would allow him to finish school before he went to war. Well, that was the plan anyway.

There were several reserves that came and talked with us – Navy and Army and others. And the Air Force sounded most interesting, so I joined the reserve – the Air Force Reserve. At the time I joined the reserve, the idea was that I would be able to graduate and then be activated into the service. But it didn't work out that way. At the end of my junior year at college, I was activated and away I went.

Vincello was trained as an armament specialist and ball turret gunner on a B-17. He was assigned to the 385th Bomb Group, 551st Squadron, in the 8th Air Force. He met the rest of his crew in Sioux City, Iowa and they trained for several months. In the spring of 1944, they flew their bomber to England. And there was more training.

Yeah, we did some training over England – getting into formations and what to do when we were in formation because we didn't want to be shooting at each other, obviously. And those were tight formations that we flew. So, it would be an easy accident to occur, but thank God for us, it didn't happen.

The tight formations were necessary for protection from enemy attacks on combat missions.

That's when I learned to admire our American fighter pilots. The German fighters – to attack us – would normally group up above us and then they would turn down and they'd come down in a string and literally, time after time, they would come right through the small holes in our formation. They'd come right on down through and, of course, they're shooting all the way. The thing that we admired and never forgot is the American fighter pilots. Our guns were shooting and there's no way to separate what you're shooting at. You're just shooting. And the American pilots would be right on their tails, coming right down through. Those fighter pilots were fantastic.

It is always nice to see a familiar face when you are far away from home. One day in London, Phil and a few buddies saw a very familiar and very famous face.

One of my most memorable experiences was being in downtown London with my buddies. No girls, just us guys. And we were getting ready to cross the street and I looked up the street and standing there with this gorgeous blonde was Jimmy Stewart, who was a pilot. And I nudged the guys and said, "Look! That's Jimmy up there!" And we all turned and crowded and looked up the way. He had planned to come our way, but he saw us gawking at him and by the time we looked back, he was galloping across the street with this lady. I can tell you one thing about Jimmy Stewart that I know for sure. He flew many missions wing to wing with our group and I know he was in some very rough rides because we were in the same place. So, they didn't select any special missions for Jimmy. He was right out there in the middle of it.

Like many fliers, Phil's crew decided to personalize their plane and give her a name.

The one that we flew the longest was called 'The West Virginian' and it got its name from a guy on our ground crew. We had a ground crew, of course, to maintain the airplane and one day the crew chief said, "We got to name the plane." We said, yeah, that's right. Let's name it. So, we all talked and none of us could decide what to name it. The crew chief was from West Virginia and we said, well, why don't we name it for you?

He said, "I don't want my name on the airplane."

"No, we're talking about West Virginia." So, we named it 'The West Virginian' and that was our first plane. And I remember the name on that one because it was an unusual experience for me – naming an airplane, you know.

Vincello's crew flew their first mission on April 26, 1944; one down and twenty-four more to go, or so they thought.

When we got there, a tour consisted of twenty-five missions. Before we got to twenty-five, they changed it to thirty. And before we got to thirty, they changed it to thirty-five.

Obviously, this didn't do much for morale. The men were quite aware that the more they flew, the greater the odds were against their survival.

Can I tell what the odds were and why it was so frustrating? We left Sioux City with thirty crews. That's ten men to a crew. That's three hundred men that went over at the time that we went. By the time they had changed the tours to where thirty-five made a tour, of those three hundred men, there were only fifteen of us left. And I thank God that I was one of them. There were only fifteen of us who actually made thirty-five missions. So it can be a little disconcerting.

The reality was, all ten men in a bomber crew rarely survived their tour of duty. Phil remembers a day when the inevitable happened.

We always flew with a flak vest on and a helmet, except in the ball turret where I couldn't wear a flak vest. The tail gunner was the youngest man on our crew. He was not nineteen yet. In his position in the tail, he would kneel back there and look out to the back. That's how he worked. Anyhow, on one of those unfortunate missions, we were really in heavy flak. And whenever we came off a target, everybody had to check in. The tail gunner did not check in. So one of the waist gunners said, "I'll go back and look." And he came back and he said, "Burnham is dead." And he and I were the only two on the crew from Massachusetts, so we had become very close friends.

So when I got up out of the ball turret, I said, "I've got to go back and see Burnham." I went back to see him and he was on his knees, which was his normal position back there, but he was slumped back and so I moved his head because I couldn't see any marks on him. I moved his head to see where he got hit. And right at the base of his skull, a sliver of flak had come up between his vest and his helmet and penetrated his brain. He didn't even bleed much. He just bled a little bit. But that's the fortune of war.

The B-17 was nicknamed 'The Flying Fortress.' There were times when it seemed that nothing could bring the bomber down.

We were up on the North Sea, bombing sub pens and we really got hit hard by the flak and the fighters. We were really in bad shape. At one point, we thought we might have to parachute out of there right into the sea and I was not very brave about that. We had pulled the door off and I looked out that door and I thought, 'Man, that's not where I want to go.' But the pilot was trying to determine which would be best for us, whether to go to a neutral country or see if we could get back to England. The decision was made that it would be better for us to go back to England.

We had one engine that was running. One had a propeller that had run away. It came right out of the nacelle and went away. A second one was not working and then we had another engine that the propeller was just flopping. To make a long story short, the pilot feathered one of the engines and we had one engine left. It took us back across the Channel, and on the coast of England there were fighter strips. None of our hydraulic systems were working, so he had to land on the belly of the plane. We took our crash positions. My position was to sit in the radio room with my back to the front. And he did a beautiful job. We hit the runway. We skidded along the runway and made quite a sound, but we landed safely and then the pilot hollered back from the cockpit, "Get out of here as fast as you can!"

What had happened was that one propeller that was windmilling hit the runway and something caused it to catch fire. So the airplane had caught fire as we were skidding on the runway and we piled out of there.

After they scrambled to safety, the crew watched their plane burn. Phil, who had just survived this incredible ordeal, thought it would be a kick to have a little fun with one of the guys who had been fighting the fire.

So we stood along the side and the ground crews went in and put out the fire and did all that stuff. And one of the members of the ground crew came up and he ended up standing right beside me. Now remember – I was a ball turret gunner. He said, "Boy, I feel so bad for that ball turret gunner."

I said, "Why? What happened to him?"

He said, "Well, you know underneath there, it's all red. There must have been just lots of blood."

The thing he didn't realize is that the hydraulic fluid that worked the ball was red. But I wasn't going to tell him anything different.

He said, "Oh, that ball turret gunner, my goodness, I feel so bad for him."

I said, "Well, I appreciate your telling me. I'll be sure and let him know." What I was really thinking was – I'm leaving you with a story you can tell when you get back to the States. But in my mind, I'm thinking that ball turret gunner you're concerned about is here telling you the story.

During one three-day span, Phil's group flew missions to Munich each day and they weren't sure why. Munich didn't have many military targets to hit. They later learned what they were aiming at.

Munich was a long air trip for us. It was down in the southeastern part of

Germany. We went down the first day and we did our bombing and there wasn't much there. There were a couple of small plants and a small air base. And lo and behold, the very next day we went back to the same target. So three days in a row, we went back to Munich and we were all puzzled. We finally found out that the reason we went to Munich three days in a row is that Hitler was having one of his famous beer garden meetings down there and we were making him happy.

On D-Day – June 6, 1944 – every available plane flew air support for the invasion of France.

We flew on D-Day, of course. That's something I'll never forget because we could see those kids on the beach. I'm saying 'kids.' We were the same age as they, but they seemed like kids to us, you know. And it just was awful to see that bombing and blasting and stuff. That mission became long because we would fly over France and then we'd head west out to the ocean and come back up the ocean to England and back to our base. The reason for that was there were so many aircraft in the air in that period, that they had to put us in some kind of a pattern so we wouldn't run into each other. D-Day for us was nothing. The Germans didn't put their fighters up and to this day, nobody knows why. So we just flew in and bombed and went around and came back.

Losing a man to flak or enemy fighters was one thing, but on one mission, Vincello's crew lost a man before they even took off. That crewman had completed more than half of his tour of duty, but on that day, he cracked. He simply could not fly. Phil and the rest of the crew wondered, 'Why now?'

We were getting ready to go on a mission. He was a good guy. It was late in the tour. And he had his hands up on the side of the door to jump in and he just froze there. I was right behind him. His name was Mike. And he had his hands up there and one foot up onto the plane. So, I slapped him and said, "Come on, Mike, let's go. We've got to get in."

And he just ... nothing moved. So I turned around to the side and looked at his face. Everything in his face was twitching. He had broken down right there. So that was the end of the ride for him.

For the rest of us, it was a little nerve-wracking because they took him away and brought in a substitute waist gunner and we had to go anyway. But the thing that worried us as we took off and headed out into the wild blue is what did he see? What caused him to break down at that moment? Did he see something that we should know about? You know, you get those strange feelings.

Between missions, the men just wanted to get their minds off flying. A little dog used to hang around the airfield and Phil's crew decided they would make him their mascot. They gave him a name and made sure his 'water' dish was always full.

And do you know what we named it? It's an Italian word, but I'll tell you what it means. It was a little black dog. We named him 'Umbriago,' which is Italian for 'drunkard.' We'd be sitting in the barracks. I'd be just drinking pop, you know, but everybody else would be drinking beer. And this dog got so he wondered what we were doing. So we said, let's give him a little bowl of this. And he used to drink beer with us until he would wobble on his legs. One of the saddest things is that when we left, we had to leave him there, so we gave him to another crew. He was great. So he earned his name, 'Umbriago.'

During their tour, Phil's crew received credit or partial credit for shooting down fifteen enemy aircraft. But there is one kill that will always stick in Vincello's mind. It came on a supply mission to France.

The clearest one that I got, the one that I clearly hit, was on one of those missions where we dropped – as a whole group – we dropped food, supplies, ammunition and stuff to the Free French in southern France. We were so far down into France that we could see the Alps – that's how far down we were. Anyhow, this thing was obviously prearranged between the Free French and the Americans. They had circles on the ground. Each plane carried different things. I forget what we had, whether it was armament or what. But the circles were colored to indicate: armament, food, supplies, you know. So as we flew down to drop those, we had to hit the right circle. And we went down very low because they wanted this stuff to land in good shape. So we dropped at a very low altitude, all of us. We went in a big circle, went down, dropped and then would start back up again. As we were starting back up again, a German fighter plane appeared, who knows from where. I mean, there was no reason for them to have them down there. But this guy appeared and he could not have been an experienced fighter pilot because he came at us from the back. The fighter pilot liked to keep speed to his advantage, so he'd either come to you from above or nose-to-

nose because the speed would close quicker. So he was coming up behind us and he was right in my gun sight. And, I saw him go down and you know what? It didn't feel good. And yet it was something that we had to do.

In the fall of 1944, Phil finally reached that magic number.

It was to Hamburg. Other than some flak and stuff, it wasn't very eventful. But it was meaningful to me because I knew that was thirty-five.

Vincello and most of his fellow crew members beat those 20-to-1 odds. They completed thirty-five missions and came home.

It isn't that we were any better. It's just fate. But yeah, we did a lot better than most.

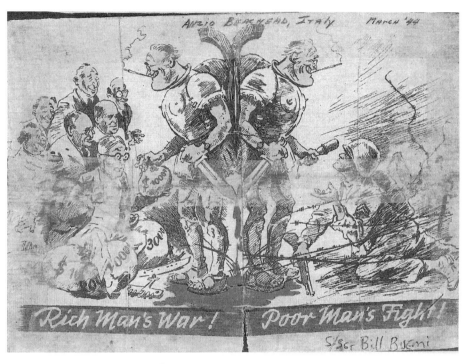

German propaganda leaflet
Courtesy of Bill Buemi

The 34th Evac Hospital participated in the war against Germany from 5 July, 1944 to 9 May, 1945. Admittances numbered 27,477 patients. The average daily admittances were ninety patients and that does not include adjustment for non-functioning time during the moves that we made. The surgical service performed 13,369 procedures and administered 11,047 anesthetics.

The mortality rate of American casualties, not including DOAs – dead on arrival – was 1.42 percent.

Ruth Penoyar Simmler
U.S. Army Nurse Corps

After she graduated from high school, Ruth Penoyar Simmler enrolled in nursing school. She was training at a hospital in Cleveland on December 7, 1941.

I took my psychiatric and contagious disease training at Cleveland City Hospital and that afternoon, I was going out to dinner with a young man and he told me what had happened that day, because actually we were kind of isolated in the hospital. I don't even know whether I saw newspapers from time to time. But he told me what had happened. It didn't really register on me – what the bombing of Pearl Harbor meant – the seriousness of it. But he knew it.

When she completed her courses, Ruth decided to become an Army nurse.

My roommate and I went up to, I think it was Port Huron Navy Station, and took our physical to get in the Army.

It is rather difficult to be modest during a military physical.

Well, I do know that my friend and I were about the only women there and we were parading around in short gowns and I can remember there was an awful lot of whistles and so forth.

But both of us had worked the night before from eleven to seven. We went up to Port Huron for our physical and came home and went back to work again at eleven o'clock that night.

Ruth was inducted into the Army on March 2, 1943.

And actually we didn't get a lot of extra training. My first assignment was Nicholl's General Hospital in Louisville, Kentucky. I was a charge nurse in a tubercular ward.

In early 1944, she was reassigned to the 100th Evacuation hospital. They shipped out on February 11, 1944.

And we went over in one of the largest convoys that had ever crossed the North Atlantic. We used to stand on deck during the day and watch all the ships. They kept changing positions constantly. That was to avoid any contact with any submarines.

After arriving in Great Britain, Ruth was reassigned to the 34th Evac Hospital.

And I was so happy. I was very fortunate to get into a very good outfit with a regular Army colonel, Kenneth Brewer, who was the commanding officer of the 34th Evac Hospital. When I went there, we were billeted in Altrincham, in private homes, and we had an awfully good time in England.

She adapted quickly to life during wartime.

We had an opportunity there to go to either Edinburgh, Scotland or to London, England. I chose to go to London and while we were there, we stayed in the Red Cross and every night we were there – we were there three nights – they had air raid warnings. Well, the first night we went from the Red Cross down to the air raid shelter and the next two nights, we just kind of ignored it and stayed in bed.

The British people were gracious hosts.

They were wonderful to us, the little bit of contact we had. Of course, when we stayed in a hotel, it was all Army personnel. But we went into town quite frequently and everyone was very friendly to us. In particular, we were out walking one day and an English policeman stopped us and he invited us to his own home for tea and we had a wonderful tea with him. And of course, when we were billeted in private homes, the families were absolutely wonderful. One family – their name was Pilkington – her husband and her son were both in the British Royal Army serving over in Africa at that time, and she was just lovely to us.

In June of 1944, the 34th Evac prepared to cross the English Channel to France.

We were moved then to a staging area in Tidworth, England. We knew that we were all set. We were equipped with chemically impregnated clothing, in case there was a chemical attack, and we were given a certain number of French francs – I think it was four hundred French francs – and a little booklet put out by the Army that gave us some knowledge of French phrases. Then they changed their mind and didn't take us. We were there two days because we heard that the channel was too rough to make a crossing.

Two and a half weeks after D-Day, they finally departed for France.

So on the 22nd of June we went aboard the SS Empire Broadsword. We crossed the English Channel and then we climbed from the large ship down a rope ladder with our musette bags on our backs and got into an LST and on the 23rd of June, D plus seventeen, we landed on Utah Beach.

The men who were already ashore were impatiently awaiting the arrival of the nurses.

But one funny thing happened. We hadn't been there very long and a Jeep with three or four naval officers pulled up and they wanted any of the nurses to go over to their – can you believe this – Officers' Club. They had a temporary Officers' Club in some tent. So, some of us took off and went. But I couldn't help but think, seventeen days after D-Day – the Navy has an Officers' Club already.

At that point, the front lines were just a few miles beyond Utah Beach.

And they had been strafing along the beach there right up to the night we came. Then, they didn't strafe and we were all safe that night. And the next day, they divided us up into groups and we joined hospitals.

Ruth was sent to a hospital in an area where some of the most intense fighting in Normandy was taking place.

We were attached to the 3rd Army and our first place we set up was Carentan and that was right near St. Lo and of course at St. Lo, they suffered a lot of casualties.

On their first day, they treated hundreds of soldiers.

We admitted over five hundred and twenty-five patients in one day. And that was when I worked in pre-op and shock. Sometimes they evacuated them directly to us from the front. Of course, the Army medics did a wonderful job in the field. But we had to check to make sure that they had a tetanus shot and to make sure they had morphine already.

That is where I really had one of my most memorable experiences. In pre-op and shock, we had to assess whether they needed surgery. Whether they could wait a while for surgery, or whether they needed immediate surgery. And we started a lot of Plasmanate there. We did a lot of things there that a nurse does. And I saw this one young captain. He was lying on a litter. I couldn't see anything wrong with him. He just was very quiet. I went to check him and to see where he had been wounded. And I turned him over and the whole back of his head was gone. You know, it was the first really traumatic thing I had seen and I'll never forget it.

According to the Geneva Convention, hospitals were to be clearly marked and should never be attacked, but some bullets came very close.

And that is where the German airplanes strafed right down the front of the road that we were on. But the Germans were pretty good about observing the red cross. All the hospital tents had red crosses – big red crosses – painted on the roofs of the tents.

Even with the occasional shooting outside her door, Ruth always felt safe.

I don't know what it is, but I never felt vulnerable and I never heard any other women talk about being scared. I always kind of felt protected. I don't know I just always assumed everything was going to be okay.

The nurses worked long days. When they got a break, any diversion was welcome.

One thing I remember particularly, I think in Carentan, there was a lot of anti-aircraft fire from our side. And we would stand there at night when the planes were going over toward England and it was actually beautiful to see the tracer bullets, which lighted up as they fired. And we thought nothing of it. At least I never did. Of course, you have to remember I was twenty-one. I wasn't as serious then as I am now.

There were many advances in medicine during the Second World War.

This is when we first started using penicillin and of course it was an absolutely wonderful thing because it saved a lot of people. But we also learned at that time that there were people that had severe allergic reactions to it. I had a patient in my ward one night that died of a penicillin reaction.

A good nurse tries to give comfort to the wounded. But sometimes remaining calm and cheerful and steady is next to impossible.

One incident I recall especially was, we were out in tents again and of course you could roll up the sides of the tents. We were out in the field so there were always plenty of flies. This is when I was working on a chest and belly ward and many of those young men had colostomies because they had bowel injuries. You just changed their colostomy dressings all day long. This one day, I went to change this young man's dressing and I opened it up. This isn't pleasant, but it was loaded with maggots. The flies had gotten in there. Well, I got so excited. I know that maggots eat necrotic tissue. But when I told the chief of surgery, he didn't seem to be too alarmed about it at all. So I just went back and used the little forceps and picked out all the maggots because I couldn't stand to look at all of them, you know. And I tried to not appear upset because I didn't want the soldier to know what I was doing.

The 34th Evacuation Hospital was always ordered to set up in a safe place – behind the lines.

At one point in time though, our hospital was three miles ahead of the Army. That was what they called an 'Army Snafu.' Do you know what 'Snafu' means? That was a 'Snafu.'

But when they were near Metz, there was no safe place for the hospital.

There were a lot of German forts right outside of Metz. I know that they did bombard the city, both in Metz and Luxembourg. They were aiming for – in Luxembourg – for this bridge that joined the old and new sections of Luxembourg, and a shell did land near the enlisted men's quarters.

In Verdun, Ruth was given a special assignment.

General Patton's aide – and I couldn't even tell you his name if I had to – came in for an appendectomy. The colonel took two of us to special nurse him. I happened to be one of the ones that was chosen. And it was ridiculous because at that time, the Army really believed in early ambulation after surgery. They realized that the patients did better if they got up and ambulated because it reduced the incidence of blood clots. But anyhow, I was with the man two nights and I was so disgusted because at that time, we had a lot of casualties in Verdun.

On one of the nights, General Patton came for a visit.

And he was very, very pleasant. I know he had an awful reputation after that slapping incident, but he was very pleasant and he told me a little story about a friend of his who had his appendix removed and he kept it in a little jar on his mantel or something like that. But after that second day, I was tired of this specialing of somebody that didn't need it, so I went to Colonel Brewer and told him I didn't think it was necessary. I wanted to get back to work again. He agreed with me and he discontinued his special nurses.

That was not the first time Ruth met Patton.

I remember going to a birthday party and I can't for the life of me remember where that was. I think it was right in Altrincham where we were or maybe we went to 3rd Army Headquarters. But I helped him cut his cake. He was so strictly GI. I have great admiration for him. Of course, being attached to the 3rd Army, we would.

During the closing months of the war, the 34th Evac began treating patients who weren't soldiers. They were survivors from the concentration camps.

We were right near Belsen, which was one of the infamous ones. I had a lot of prisoners of war there and of course they were all suffering from nutritional deficiencies. They could not eat food for quite a while, so we gave them all Plasmanate. And I used to come on duty and there would be maybe twenty-five or thirty of them that I'd have to go along down the row. They didn't speak English and I didn't speak their language. But I'd start Plasmanate on them. That is what we were doing until they could graduate to liquids and then on to soft and then solid food. After I would stick them with this big needle that you'd give Plasmanate with, some of them would just smile and pat me on the arm, you know.

Most veterans believe their time in service was well worth it, but it was a tough life.

We were billeted in little pyramidal tents and my buddy, Iris, and I had a tent. There was a little stove in the center of it. We'd both work the same shift and we'd come off duty and we'd pick up some firewood. I think they did put firewood out in front of our tents. We'd stoke up our little stove and we'd go to bed. And we would put the metal part of our helmets on the stove to heat water. I never wore the metal part. I maybe wore my helmet liner, but I didn't wear my helmet on duty because the patients wouldn't have had them. But I can remember heating water to bathe, in my metal helmet. I would first of all, take a bath, then I remember washing my pants and bra in the same water. Then, I'd brush my teeth and spit in the helmet and then we'd throw it out the front door. That was the way we lived. It was kind of rough, but I don't remember being overly stressed by it.

Giving in to stress was not an option.

You know, that was not a word that we used too much at that time. This may sound fatuous, but I have to tell you it just didn't enter our minds. We worked twelve noon to twelve midnight. Or the other shift, twelve midnight to twelve noon. The nurses chose that. We could have worked seven to seven, but we didn't choose to. None of the nurses went home, but toward the end there were three or four that were diagnosed with rheumatic fever and arthritis. We were out in the field and it was freezing cold. I remember in several areas there was snow on the ground.

In spite of the conditions, they did their job and the 34th Evacuation Hospital had a survival rate of nearly 99 percent. Thanks to nurses like Ruth Simmler, a lot of young men came home.

I never enjoyed taking care of patients as much as I did the patients that came through in the Army. I mean, you know, they needed our help.

This diary is one of the first submissions I received when I began collecting personal histories of World War Two. Peter Mihalic was seventeen when he enlisted in the Marines. He doesn't write about it in his diary, but his foot became infected while he was on Guadalcanal, and after a short stay in Australia he was sent back to the States.

Peter was a gifted, natural writer. This is his personal account of one of the most intense campaigns of the war in the Pacific.

Peter M. Mihalic
USMC
Field Book Notes: Guadalcanal

Today, approximately four months after the landing of the First Marine Division on the island of Guadalcanal, I sit here reflecting over the action they have seen to date. A lot can happen to us here.

First of all I guess I have to explain who I am and what outfit I'm with on this Island. My name is Peter Michael Mihalic, a Private First Class in the Marine Corps and I am attached to the communications section of Option Battery of the Fifth Battalion of the Eleventh Marines. The battalion has three batteries and H & S, (Headquarters and Service). Each battery has 4 guns. They are one hundred five-millimeter howitzers. A fairly big gun, it is the equivalent of the naval 4 inch gun. But, whereas the naval gun has a flat trajectory, ours is more like a mortar. We can drop our shells over hills and obstacles, which a naval gun cannot do. Ours was the heaviest artillery on the Island when we first landed here on that eventful and fateful seventh day of August in the year of Nineteen Hundred Forty-Two.

Now I will go on and repeat some of the highlights of the action and fighting on Guadalcanal.

To date, we have had approximately 150 official air raids. That is that Japanese bombers have come over and dropped their bombs, or Jap Zeros have come over and strafed us.

We have been shelled by a Jap battleship twice with fourteen or sixteen-inch shells. Both shellings lasted about four hours. Those fourteen-inch shells weigh about one ton and I cannot describe the loudness of the explosion. It is something one has to go through oneself to be able to appreciate the experience. It is indescribable.

We were shelled about five times by submarines, three or four times by a cruiser and a few times by destroyers. As I said before, one has to go through these experiences to get the full benefit of them.

We have had seven major battles with the Japs on this Island. The first was the

Battle of Red Beach. The second was Bloody Knoll. The third was some hundred yards south of Bloody Knoll. The fourth was approximately two miles west of the former. The fifth took place three miles east of the former. The sixth was the Battle of the Matanikau River. The seventh took place one mile west of the Matanikau River. In all these battles our artillery was the most potent factor in the winning of the battles.

Now I will try to relay more fully in detail each event in the order it happened.

Morning of August seventh. The first troops to go over the side were the Infantry. They cleaned the beach of Japs and pushed as far inland as the other side of the airfield, which was approximately one mile from the beach. Meanwhile a few (amphibious) planes circled the Island spotting Jap positions and relaying same to the Infantry. In that way the beach and the airfield were soon clear of Japs and the rest of our troops were ready to move in.

Two hours after the Infantry hit the beach, we, the artillery, went over the side. Regardless, if the Infantry had cleared the beach or not, the artillery would have to move in anyway. Everything was timed. God only knows what would have happened had the Infantry not cleared the beach so we could land the artillery.

The Japs were completely defeated and Guadalcanal was ours, for the time being. Little did we realize what the future held in store for us. The Japanese were not going to let such an important air base slip through their fingers and not put up a fight for it. Oh no! That morning Japanese bombers, dive-bombers and Zeros came over and attacked our ships in the bay. Our ships shot down a good many of them and the only harm they did was damage one of our transports so badly that she had to be beached and then unloaded. She was the Eliot. We did not have a fighter plane in the area and were not to have any for eleven more days, though we knew that not.

That night most of our ships pulled out after being unloaded. A few remained to finish unloading in the morning and most of the night.

Meanwhile, we were setting up our positions around the airfield. We set up the guns and hauled in our gear and always were on the alert for Jap snipers, for they were numerous. A few of our men were killed by these snipers and we had to send patrols out to ferret them out. Next morning the few of our ships that were still in the bay were attacked again by bombers and dive-bombers. Our ships shot down a few of the planes and no damage was done to the ships.

But that day we Marines got our first taste of a bombing raid on us, for those Jap bombers dropped a good sized load on us. Obviously they were trying to hit the airfield, so that our planes couldn't land, but, alas, their aim was not exactly accurate, for many a stray bomb dropped a good way from the airfield and in and among our troops. Many a Marine was killed due to a Jap bombardier's inaccurate aim. The irony of it all.

We soon came to learn to expect the Jap bombers about noontime, for without fail, when they came, they came at midday.

Meantime, all the Infantry were still shoving the Japs farther and farther back. They did a grand job and the Island was fairly secure from Jap land attacks.

Now the reader must be given to understand that for eleven days, up until August eighteenth, we had not a single fighter plane in our area. Therefore, after our ships pulled out and the Jap bombers commenced concentrating on us, why, all we could do was watch as they came over with only a few feeble bursts of A.A. to hamper them. Now there isn't anything in this world that the Marines hate more than something that they can't fight back. No fighter planes, no satisfaction of knowing that some of the bombers would never see their base again. No, only a sickening and helpless feeling when bombs are dropping. And Marines hate to feel helpless. The reigning question for the next eleven days was, "Where are our planes?" The airfield is in readiness to receive them. What the big delay was, few people knew.

The next day our outfit moved up to the positions we still occupy. We began moving late in the evening and we had to bivouac on the beach for the night. That night we heard the thunderous roar of a gigantic naval battle out at sea. We never got a report on it though. I'd give one hundred dollars to know the results of that battle.

Next morning we moved into our position, set up everything, went about making the place halfway livable and sent out a few patrols to rout any snipers that may have been in the vicinity. This position of ours was about one half-mile east from the first airfield, Henderson Field, or the Bomber Strip, as we call it.

The beach on Guadalcanal faces to the north. A few yards from the beach is a magnificent coconut tree plantation that is about five hundred yards wide and stretches lengthwise for miles from east to west. Just inland from the coconut trees where the trees end, there is an open field that is about one quarter mile wide and runs for miles *lengthwise from east to west. Inland from the field is a strip of woods on the northern fringe of which is our position, facing the bay. The bomber field was a half mile from us and the smooth open field that was destined to hold our fighter planes was approximately five hundred yards distant, to the right of us. In other words our position was between the two bomb targets, the bomber field and the fighter field. Consequently, all inaccurately aimed Jap bombs, if they did not fall to the other side of the airfields, they fell in or around us. And that is why, after we learned all this, that a bombing raid struck a note of terror in the hearts of the Artillery men.*

For eleven days, we withstood a bombing raid a day, without even a single fighter plane to offer any opposition. For eleven days our engineers kept patching up the holes in the airfield made by the bombers. For eleven days we asked the questions, "Where are our planes? When are they coming?" There were a few men who just could not stand the strain of the air raids day after day and finally ended up just a human jumble of nerves. I believe that if we had the planes to offer resistance, these men would never have cracked. For with planes, there would always be the hope that our planes would drive the bombers away. As it was, it was inevitable that we have at least one raid a day, unless for unfavorable weather conditions. Unfortunately, the elements seemed to favor them at the time.

On the average about 25 bombers would come over and drop their loads. So many bombs were dropped on this Island that one of our aviators, when he came in said, I quote, "Gee, this place looks like a sieve from the air", unquote. Those were the results of only the first eleven days of bombing. I should also say that our A.A. guns brought down a few of the bombers. So much for the air activity of the first eleven days.

Meanwhile, I can't recall the exact day the Battle of Red Beach took place.

The First Marine Regiment (Infantry) had set up about a mile northeast of the bomber field. Out of nowhere, or so it seems, emerge about one thousand Japs. They came marching down the beach from the east towards us and the airfield one moonlit night. They stumbled right into the First Marines and a terrific battle ensued. The seventy-five millimeter pack howitzer outfit (Third Battalion Eleventh) was called upon to fire on the Japs that night. They did a magnificent job that night with the Infantry cleaning up all the artillery didn't get. The battle was over before morning. When dawn came, there, strewn about on the beach, were eight hundred seventy dead Japanese. Only two Jap prisoners were taken and they, only as a source of information for our officers. The Marines took no prisoners if they could help it. The Marines collected plenty of Jap souvenirs, like rifles, pistols, flags and miscellaneous articles, in fact, anything Japanese. Some even pulled the gold teeth out of the dead Japs' mouths. The Marines from then on were souvenir happy. After every battle they collected Jap articles.

The morning after, the Jap prisoners we already had were put to the task of burying their own dead. There was a nauseating stink coming from the beach for the next two weeks.

An interesting thing about that first battle, very few of the Japs carried rifles. Most of them had knee mortars and grenades. We were soon to learn that the Japs are noted for their mortars. They prefer them to artillery I imagine. In every battle with them they always had plenty of mortars.

Morning after the battle, the artillery was credited with eighty five percent of the Japs and our General sent them a Letter of Commendation. The Marines suffered very few casualties. The artillery won the respect of the Infantry and vice versa, everyone's morale was boosted a little by our victory, the General was proud of us and everyone was fairly happy for awhile.

Somewhere in those first eleven days we were shelled once by a cruiser and once by a submarine. The cruiser came in to shell us one night about twelve o'clock. It sent one of its observation planes ahead of it, the plane dropped flares where he wanted the shells and the cruiser put them there. The cruiser shelled and the plane dropped his flares for about three or four hours, and then as a parting gesture, the plane let loose some bombs and went his way again, then left us in peace once more. A cruiser puts out some five and eight-inch shells and they can do a lot of damage. I don't recall if anyone was hurt that night, but I do recall that it was a mighty uncomfortable night.

The submarine pooped out a few shells without the help of a plane. I doubt if he scared anyone, because subs carry very small guns. In comparison with a cruiser or other ship, a sub's guns sound like peashooters.

That about covers the first eleven days. I've omitted most of the minor details *for it would take a year of writing to cover everything. I'm just trying to relay the things most important as I recall them.*

August eighteenth was a day of rejoicing for us Marines. At approximately six o'clock in the morning, twenty Navy Grumman Wildcat fighter planes, fresh off an aircraft carrier circled the airfield and one by one came in to land. All the Marines on the Island came out of their foxholes to watch the spectacle. At last, our planes! Now let the Jap bombers come, we thought. The bombers came as usual, but now it was a different story. Instead of flying nonchalantly over us and dropping their loads, they had something to worry about up there. Many was the Jap bomber that never saw his home base, after coming over the next day. For the next three weeks, those twenty planes of ours did a superhuman job of downing the Japs as they came over day after day.

Naturally, some of our fighters were shot down and at the end of the third week, I believe we had four or five of the original twenty in fighting condition.

I must also mention that when our twenty fighter planes came here, about ten Navy dive-bombers came in also. But these planes could not be used for fighters, for their top speed is only between one hundred fifty and one hundred seventy-five miles per hour. They were strictly a dive-bomber. They carried three bombs, one five-hundred pound bomb and two two-hundred-fifty pounders. They were of great service to us also. They would patrol out over the bay and when a Jap ship was spotted they would do their work. These planes saw a lot of action, too, and in three weeks, I believe, we had but one left.

During these three weeks, we were shelled again by a cruiser, a submarine and a destroyer. Each one shelled us on different nights. Our dive-bombers could not go out to get them for the nights were pitch dark. Their objective this time seemed to be the airfield where our planes were. All three shellings lasted approximately three hours. From the reports I received, only minor damages were inflicted on some of the planes. Damages easily fixed. We got a few reports in that our Navy sank the Jap cruiser the morning after it shelled us. Reports never confirmed.

Meantime, the Infantry and our artillery had a hot time of it. The Japs, nightly, were landing small forces of men on the Island to the east and west of us. Almost nightly a skirmish would be raging between Marines and Japs to the east or west of us.

Every time a few Japs would land, the commanding General would send out some men to wipe them out or scatter them, for fear that they might organize with those Japs already on the Island. We were called upon to fire a few times at small forces of them landing. General Tojo must have been in a quandary wondering what happened to the men he sent to Guadalcanal.

The bombings continued as usual. Bombers came over incessantly day after day. Then after that third week we got a few more fighters and some more dive-bombers. That was another day of celebration for us, for as I've said before, we only had five fighters in flying condition left, and things were looking gloomy again. At the time, we all wished that these new fighters would do as swell a job as the first twenty. We needn't have worried, for they proved themselves capable.

Bombers came over as usual and our fighters would go up to meet them. When our planes failed to drive them away, the Japs came over the Island at a cost of about twenty out of twenty-five bombers shot down. The only regret I had at the time was that the Japs usually got to drop their bombs before our fighters got on their tails to take their toll.

The new dive-bombers we got in saw a little action in the next few days, too. A few Jap ships strayed in to try and land supplies for their troops here, and the dive-bombers went out to get them. A few of the Jap ships would get in at night though and land their supplies and our planes would be helpless, because they couldn't take off without lighting the airfield, and we couldn't turn on the lights for fear that a Jap warship accompanying the supply ship would open up on the perfect target of lights. But usually our planes would take off at daybreak and overtake the ships out at sea and more often than not those ships would never see another port. During this time we were shelled again. First of all a destroyer shelled us one night for about three hours. No damage was done, however. All he accomplished was keeping us in our foxholes while the shells flew. The next night a cruiser and submarine both went to work on us. A few of the cruiser's shells did a little damage on the airfield, minor damages to a few planes and ruined the gear of a few outfits. They accomplished about the same thing the destroyer did the night before, kept us in our foxholes.

Now I come to one of the episodes on this Island, one that I remember most vividly and shall never forget.

About eleven o'clock on the night of September thirteenth, a Jap battleship pulled into the bay and went about giving us the worst shelling we ever had on the Island and with the biggest guns. For three and one-half hours he lay out there throwing fourteen and sixteen inch shells at us. It was the most hellish night we went through on the Island. They literally strafed us with sixteen-inch shells that night. Next morning after the check up it wound up that six or seven of our fighters were completely demolished and six dive-bombers ditto. Quite a number of men were killed and lots of equipment demolished. All in all it was a nightmarish night for every man on the Island.

The next night the second of the battles took place about two hundred yards behind our position. And we were the heaviest artillery on the Island then. The Fifth Marine Regiment had set defenses behind us and were all ready to receive the Japs. At about eleven o'clock that night they attacked and a few minutes later, the second of the Bloody Battles was in full swing. Machine gun fire, the Japs' inevitable mortars, our mortars and our artillery, all these noises were merged together into a great noise, such as I have never in my life before heard, and I hope I am fortunate enough never to hear again. The Japs screaming their blood thirsty battle cry, "Blood for the Emperor," and the Marines cutting them down with machine guns and yelling "Here's to that bastard Tojo," sounds like these were heard that night just two hundred yards behind us. Our artillery moved into the field that night and began putting our shells right over our positions and into the Japs. Each of the guns in our battery shot thirteen hundred rounds that night at a range of less than three hundred yards. All night the four guns shot a grand total of fifty two hundred rounds. The Japs went insane when we started in with our guns. From where we were we could hear them yelling, "Stop the artillery, please, stop the artillery." Japs are mortally afraid of artillery, and after that night their fear was increased about tenfold. The battle lasted till daybreak and at that time what was left of the Japs took off for the hills. In the morning there lay about five hundred dead Japs, a good three hundred killed by our artillery and God knows how many were wounded, but strong enough to crawl away. A few patrols went out to ferret out any snipers that might still be hanging around. That morning was a scramble for souvenirs; the front lines were full of men taking souvenirs from the dead Japs. From papers found on some of them we learned that they were Jap Imperial Marines, the

Emperor's own outfit. We also found out that they were veterans of attacks on other islands, for many of them had American Marine souvenirs, such as pictures of a Marine and his family, or girl friend or American money or Marine shoes and clothes. When first I saw the dead Japs I was a little inclined to feel sorry for them, but after I found what they were carrying, my sympathy for them turned to rage and I vowed if I found any wounded Japs I would run them through with a bayonet or put a bullet through their thick skulls. Our men captured a Jap officer that night and he requested that before we kill him to let him see our <u>automatic</u> artillery. That'll give the reader an idea of how fast we fired our guns that night. He also said that the Marines fought unfairly, that they only fought for souvenirs. It was the opinion of most of the men that the Jap battleship shelling us the night before was the prelude to this battle. The object of this attack, obviously, was to take the airfield. It also seemed that the Japs were pretty confident of the attack, for the next Jap planes, six in all, tried to land on the field. They never knew what hit them. Oh yes, the Marines called this the 'Battle of Bloody Knoll.' The Nips' blood made excellent fertilization for the land back there. Again, we had to inhale a nauseating stink for a few days.

The Jap bombers came over as usual and our planes kept fighting them. When the Japs weren't driven away they came over and dropped their loads at the extremely high price of fifteen or twenty of their twenty-five or thirty bombers shot down. Three out of four times they got over to drop their bombs, though. The bombs usually killed quite a few men, very seldom hit the airfield, and scared the pants off us. They took a toll of ten men from our battalion all in all. Within the next few nights, we were shelled again by a sub, and a couple destroyers. Again, the most they accomplished was ruining a few outfits' gear, putting a few small holes in the airfield, a few slight damages to planes, scare us a little, and kept us in our foxholes and from sleep.

Then the thing we hoped for most happened. Every day we got a few new fighter planes and dive-bombers in. Soon we would have a fleet of fighters in and the bombers would come no more. The number of planes kept building up and at one point we had as high as forty-five fighters in flying condition.

The dive-bombers were doing a good job, too. They were steadily increasing the number of Jap ships sunk around this area.

Now, one more horrible night. At ten minutes of twelve on the night of October thirteenth, once more a Jap battleship pulled into the bay and began to throw fourteen and sixteen inch shells at us. It was a repetition of the previous shellings by a battleship. This one did a little better job on our planes, killed quite a few men and ruined more gear. The reader can take the explanation I gave of the first battleship shelling and apply it to this one and save me a lot of words. Our commanding staff was so worried about a Jap landing party and that the Jap ship might do irreparable damage to us, that the General sent out an S.O.S. to our Navy to come in to help us. In truth, the Japs did land quite a few men that night on the west side of the Island. Two nights later, from what I understand, you people at home heard the news commentators say that the situation was grave on Guadalcanal. It certainly was, for awhile. Now that Jap reinforcements came to the Island we were expecting a battle any day. Eventually they would organize and attack.

We kept getting in new planes till the number of fighters was raised to sixty and the dive-bombers, twenty-five. The Jap bombers came over less often now and two out of four times got to drop their loads on us. After they dropped their bombs, more often than not, all of them were shot down and all of them were quoted as calling this 'Death Island' for hardly any of their fellows ever came back after coming here on a bombing mission. Very shortly, we thought, we would have no more air raids, because of the number of planes we had. Added to this was the rumor that very shortly we would receive some Lockheed Interceptors, the double fuselage plane, that was capable of going up to meet the bombers and break them up before they got here. They have a speed of five hundred M.P.H. and can go as high as any bomber. With these planes, never would we have to worry about bombings.

The attack we had been expecting finally came. It happened about twelve o'clock one night about three hundred yards southeast of Bloody Knoll. The Japs attacked our Seventh Marine Infantry regiment and the third of the Bloody Battles took place. Again, we heard those terrible screams and explosions, but very faintly this time. Our artillery had a big hand in this battle, too. I don't recall the number of rounds we fired that night, but what we did fire seemed to be sufficient. The next morning, after a night of furious fighting, over five hundred dead Japs were counted and quite a few wounded ones that the inevitable souvenir hunters later killed. A great number of the Japs' favorite weapons (mortars) were captured. Quite a number of our men were killed that night due to that weapon. For the third successive time the Japs were completely beaten by us on this Island. The Infantry praised us and vice-versa and all was well again except for the men who lost their buddies in the battle. Now we wondered where and when the Japs were going to try again. They would, we knew.

The bombers continued to come over until the early part of November. The last time they came over, I believe, was on November seventh. A few days before, what we had all hoped for finally came true, for one evening twelve Interceptors circled our field and came in to land. That was another day of rejoicing for the Marines on Guadalcanal. The bombers came as usual on November seventh, but that time they must have decided that our Interceptors were just a little bit too much for them to handle. Since then we haven't had one air raid, except for a few night bombings which I'll explain later. During November we got a few more fighters and dive-bombers in and eight more Interceptors. That raised the total to twenty Interceptors, sixty Grumman fighters, and twenty-five dive-bombers. I must also say that we had six torpedo planes, too. They also were very effective on the Jap ships that were in this area. Also, quite a few Flying Fortresses began landing here. They were using this as a base to bomb the Jap occupied islands of the Solomons.

I forgot to mention one episode that happened in the latter part of September. We had forty-five fighters in flying condition and had a sufficient amount of gasoline to keep them in the air to meet the bombers. Then Dugout Doug MacArthur's Flying Fortresses began to stop over here during a bombing flight and they used our gas and bombs. The Flying Fortresses use a considerable amount of gas, they take on three thousand gallons I believe, and after a week of their landing here we underwent a serious gas shortage. Fact is, at one time we had only enough gas to send about five planes up and the Japs had a few field days over here. Then a few days later a couple of our supply ships came in and we worked furiously day and night to unload the gasoline. Many is the officer I saw that day that shed a lot of sweat right along with the enlisted men unloading gasoline.

Well, those Flying Fortresses didn't do any more stopping over at this Island any more, not until the latter part of October. Then, we had gotten in a good supply of gas, enough to fill their huge tanks and our fighters, too.

I also forgot to mention that in the latter part of September we had both airfields working. The bombers and dive-bombers and torpedo planes landed at the Bomber Strip, as we call it, and the fighters on the Fighter Strip. I have already given the location of these earlier in the narrative.

After the battleships had shelled us and the Japs landed men, a little later the battle of Bloody Knoll took place, which I have already related. Well, a few days later, the middle of October, the Japs again began attempting to land troops. Nearly every night from mid October to the first of November, the Japs tried to land. They didn't succeed every time, fortunately for us, due to our Navy. The Japs had a system when they attempted to land. They would sneak a troopship and supply ship into the bay under cover of night, along with a few warships, usually a cruiser and a couple of destroyers. Then the warships would commence to shell us to draw our attention away from the west of the Island, where the Japs were landing. A plane from the cruiser would inch above and drop flares on us and the ships would fire where the flare was dropped. This would go on for a couple of hours until the Japs landed. The plane, without fail, would drop his load of bombs. He was given the adequate name of 'Good Time Charlie'. At daybreak, after the naval shelling, our dive-bombers would go up and try to overtake the ships out at sea. Usually, they'd overtake them and sink or seriously damage some of them. Even if they didn't, we would intercept them out there, somewhere. As I've said before, this continued till the beginning of November.

Now that we knew the Japs were landing we began wondering where they would attack after they organized. Our dive-bombers and Air Cobras were continually bombing their supplies and strafing the men, respectively, so we did not think they would be in good condition when they did attack. About the twentieth of October, the first attack came. In the middle of one night the Japs attacked the Seventh Marine Infantry Regiment again, about two miles southwest of our position in the rear of the airfield and the fourth of the Bloody Battles ensued. We were called upon to fire again that night and fire we did and made a good job of it. The Japs would not break through our lines and at daybreak the fighting ceased.

Again the Japs were completely defeated in their fourth big attempt to take the airfield. I don't recall the count on the number of dead Japs, in fact, I don't recall getting a count, anyhow, again, the Infantry praised the Artillery and vice-versa and the souvenir hunters had a field day and all was well again, for awhile. At this point the

Japs were still landing troops and we all looked forward to still another battle. It came sooner than we expected. A few nights later the Japs tried again. This time about three miles east of the scene of the Bloody Knoll Battle. They attacked the First Marines for the second time and the fifth of the Bloody Battles took place. We did our job well, the Infantry did theirs well and the Japs were repulsed again by daybreak. I did not get a report on the number of dead Japs this time either. Quite a number were killed though. Again the Infantry praised...etc. The souvenir fanatics had another field day, too.

The Japs in one of their landing parties managed to get a few tanks and a few big guns ashore. The tanks were to play a part in the next battle and I'll commence to tell about the guns. They landed one six-inch naval gun and a couple seventy-millimeter artillery pieces. Well, the big gun opened up on us one morning and for two weeks he kept up the same system which consisted of firing about ten shots in the general direction of the airfield during the three meal times of the day. Unfortunately, at times his aim was accurate and many a shell landed in our battalion area. The shells killed a few men in our battalion. The airfield was sending up dive-bombers every day to try and locate his position, but it appears he was too well camouflaged for they never found him. It took an Infantry patrol to finally get him. They found five thousand rounds laying next to the gun. If they hadn't captured it, that gun would still be firing on us. The seventy-millimeter pieces that landed opened fire on us one day, but he didn't fire long. Our whole regiment of artillery opened up on them and annihilated all their guns.

By this time, some of the Army from New Caledonia came to the Island. They brought along seven, one hundred fifty five-millimeter rifles. That is, they were coastal guns and they fire the same as a naval gun, with a flat trajectory. Some Army Infantry came, but they were not put into action right off.

Now we come to the sixth Bloody Battle. The Japs had organized their forces again and with the help of ten tanks they attacked again. Part of our First, Fifth and Seventh Marines had set up defenses on the east side of the Matanikau River. This night the Japs attempted to cross the river, break through our lines and advance on the airfield. Their tanks may have gotten through if it weren't for our artillery. The tanks were crossing the river when we were called upon to fire. We knocked out eight of the tanks while they were still in the river. After that we began firing on the Japs' lines. We did a good job, the Infantry did a very good job and the Japs were vanquished again. The usual procedure followed again – the artillery praising the Infantry, etc. The souvenir fanatics had another field day and the artillery was commended by the Commanding General for knocking out the tanks. All was well again for awhile.

We knew that there were still quite a few Japs on the west of the island and wondered if and when they'd try again.

Our Infantry moved up to a mile west of the river and set up a base there. Well, one night, those damned persistent Japs tried again. They attacked in the middle of the night and the final of the Bloody Battles ensued. The Infantry and the Artillery did a royal job on them this last time and really showed them they were licked. They were beat decisively that time and their troops scattered. Now the Infantry sends out patrols every day to ferret out the few Japs that are left. The Japs on the Island now are completely stranded. Their ships can't get in to bring them supplies and eventually they will starve to death or be killed or captured by the Marines. Our Air Cobras and dive-bombers go out periodically to strafe and bomb them. They are doomed, what is left of them. All this happened before November thirteenth.

Now one evening in November we got some startling news. Our Commander told us that a convoy of Jap ships, approximately seventy in all, were headed our way! Nothing scared us as much as the possibility that we might be shelled again by a battleship, for there were two in the convoy. We were certain that our Navy was out there and we prayed that they and our dive-bombers and torpedo planes would stop them. We needn't have worried, for we have a bunch of fighting gobs on our side. That night our Navy made contact with their convoy and a super terrific naval battle took place. We could see the flashes and hear the booms of the battle from the Island. It lasted all night. Our dive-bombers and torpedo planes were taking off all night and together with the Navy they did a grand job on the convoy. A few nights later you people at home heard your news commentator tell about the terrific naval battle off Guadalcanal in which one battleship was sunk and another seriously damaged. Three cruisers sunk, eight transports sunk. Four supply ships sunk. And a considerable number of destroyers sunk. And a great number of other ships seriously damaged. All these casualties the Japs suffered. That is the report you people received. On the Island here, our pilots told us that all in all, sixty Jap ships were sunk. Our Navy slaughtered them that night. I believe we lost something like fifteen ships. That was the night that our cruiser, San Francisco, did such a heroic job on the Japs. The news commentators told about that over the radio.

Well now that the convoy was destroyed, the Island was fairly secure. The Japs had fought all they're going to fight with the Marines on Guadalcanal. The Army began to bring troops here to relieve the Marines. We have about seventy-five fighter planes, thirty dive-bombers, twenty Air Cobras, six torpedo planes, and twenty Interceptors here now. No Jap planes can come close to here now. Army Flying Fortresses land here regularly and quite a few use this as a base to bomb islands occupied by Japs. New Zealand bombers even stop off here. Yes, this is a regular operations base for the Navy and bombers now. The Army have relieved nearly all the Marine outfits of the First Marine Division. They are taking our positions and we are just standing by, marking time, till a transport comes to take us off this Island, to where, I don't know. Well, the Marines took this Island from the Japs, now it's up to the Army to hold on to it. Let's hope they can do as good a job holding as we did taking it.

Well, that's that. I've tried my best to write down all the important things that have happened since the day we landed on the Island. I'm no Poe or Longfellow or Shaw. I wish I was, but anyway, I've tried my best to tell everything.

After four months on this Island every day under fire, one would think that a man would feel bitter about everything, but strangely enough, I only feel a kind of satisfaction that I have had my crack at the Japs and I also feel glad that I was one of those chosen twelve thousand, that first landed on this Island and took this strategic Pacific base from the Japs.

During those four months, or should I say, during those first three months, we lived as no dog should even live. After one day's raid, we lived in constant dread of the next day's inevitable raid, thanking God that we weren't killed in this raid and praying that we'd live thru the next one. It is a horrible thing to be in a foxhole while bombs are raining around you. A feeling so horrible, that I won't endeavor to describe it to you.

I have been up in the front lines with the Infantry four times. The artillery must have an observation post, a place of vantage from where an officer directs their fire. These are usually right on the front lines. I was there as a communications man to monitor communications between the observation post and the artillery. The first three times nothing happened, just saw a few Japs off in the distance. We also got some good looks at our Air Cobras and dive-bombers strafing and bombing them. The fourth time I was up there, from November twenty-seventh to December first, things started popping. On the evening of November thirtieth, the Japs began shelling us with mortars and field pieces. They kept up the barrage on the hill where we were all night. I was in a foxhole with a naval ensign who was up with us to gain experience to direct naval gunfire. He and I stayed in that hole all night in the rain, while shells were hitting all around us. We missed death by a few feet many times that night. Commissioned officer or not, before morning came I knew all about him and he knew all about me. When two men are under shellfire in a foxhole, rank means nothing. We were not Ensign Pray and PFC Mihalic, we were just two men with the fear of death in us. I'll never forget that night and I believe he won't either.

Many of the Marines collected a lot of Jap souvenirs while here, but I haven't taken any. I believe that when a Jap is dead, that's all I want out of him, his life, for being on the other side. I believe that's enough to ask of a man. Another reason is because in later life I don't want to be reminded of my stay on Guadalcanal. I've been thru four months of war, every day under fire and you can take my word for it, believe me, War is Hell.

Modern people claim to be civilized, but I can't see any civilization in a war.

This about concludes everything I have to say about our stay on Guadalcanal.

Today is Saturday...

Richard Francies at the World War Two Memorial in 2004

Jean Hacker in Hawaii (1943)

Clarence Swope and Clayton Rippey

Anthony Adams

The crew of the Constant Nymph

Ruth Simmler (left) in France

American propaganda leaflet dropped on Okinawa
Courtesy of George Schlee

Well, I think I was really our secret weapon because I was in two first wave landings. One in the Philippines – Leyte in October of '44 – and the second one was Okinawa. And as the Japs saw me feeling my way ashore, they died laughing saying, 'Here comes Blind Wendell.'

Richard Wendell Johnson

U.S. Army

In 1941, Wendell Johnson was a freshman at Harvard. After the attack on Pearl Harbor, he tried to enlist.

But I was unable to do so because my eyes, without glasses, are so poor that the Navy wouldn't take me and the Army wouldn't take me and the Air Force wouldn't take me. Nobody would take me.

Johnson stayed in school until June of 1943 when he was drafted into 'limited service.' After induction, he joined the Army Specialized Training Program. In the fall, the soldiers in his A.S.T.P. unit formed a football team. One of Wendell's teammates later became a football legend.

A fella named Lou Groza, who had been at Ohio State, was there also. So I was center and he was right guard and we had a pretty good football team at that A.S.T.P. unit.

In 1944, the Army needed men in the fight and they closed the A.S.T.P.

The whole 6th Service Command, which was Ohio, Michigan and Illinois, was sent out to Oregon to the 96th Division. And I was magically changed from 'limited service' to Class A at the stroke of a pen.

Johnson joined the 383rd Regiment, I Company in the 96th Division. They shipped out in October of 1944. Their destination was Leyte in the Philippines.

And so we landed on October 20th (1944). It wasn't a serious landing. It wasn't a tough landing in that it wasn't like the Marines on Iwo Jima or Tarawa or anything. There weren't as many Japanese there in the Philippines. That's one of the reasons they picked that island of Leyte, because it was lightly held. So we didn't have a whole lot of casualties. The biggest hazard there was the swamps. We went inland through the swamps and it was just – you know, knee-high, hip-high, mud. And we finally got into dry land about five miles inland, but then they couldn't get supplies to us because there were no roads through the swamps. The other thing that happened was that the Japanese Navy came in and there was the Battle of Leyte Gulf, the biggest naval battle of World War Two. Fortunately, we beat the Japanese, but that chased away all of our supply ships and so, for two weeks, those of us who were inland lived on three things: One was coconuts, one was Indian corn, and the third was sugar cane. And I lost about thirty pounds, just on that diet. But, you know, when you're hungry enough, you'll eat what you can.

For nearly six months, Johnson fought in the mountains of Leyte.

I've got a couple of memories of being up there. A lot of dead Japanese – they were along the trail and there were skulls and whatnot. Also, it was cold up there and we had long leeches. They were about six inches long. So when you had a foxhole up there, you had to watch out for the leeches because they could attach to your skin. You'd burn them off with cigarettes.

Many of the casualties in the Philippines were from tropical diseases.

A lot of sickness up there. We lost more to sickness than to Japanese bullets on Leyte. You had things like ringworm and hookworm and strombladies, and yellow jaundice and dengue fever. And those were normal kinds of things.

In the spring of 1945, the 96th Division left Leyte for their next assignment – the invasion of Okinawa.

The landing was April 1, 1945 – April Fool's Day – and a few days before we landed, I was told that I was going to be the new flame-thrower operator for I Company. How do they do this? I don't know who the former guy was, but I had no instruction and no instruction manual. The darn thing weighs eighty-two pounds when it's fully loaded and they said, "Okay, Johnson, you're the flame-thrower operator." That's it.

I said, "Well, I'd like to try it off the stern."

"Oh no, you'll burn up the ship."

I had no practice and here I am, going ashore on Okinawa.

Fortunately for Wendell, he didn't need to use the flame-thrower on the first day.

We didn't get a whole lot of fire, but it was a magnificent spectacle on April 1st when we were going ashore in these 'Alligators' and here are the battleships and the cruisers and the aircraft carriers and they were all firing right over our heads. It was a huge amount of sound.

The Japanese didn't put up much resistance to the initial landings on Okinawa, but that was their plan. Their strategy was to allow the troops to come ashore and concentrate their defenses on the southern half of the island.

Three or four days later, we pivoted and turned south – the 96th Division did – and we ran into the first opposition. We came to a really rocky, cliff-like kind of thing called Kakazu Ridge and this held us up for more than a week. We took a lot of casualties attacking Kakazu Ridge. Well, sort of alongside of it – along the ocean – there were a lot of rocky outcroppings from which the Japanese were machine-gunning us. At first it took us by surprise, and then we really had to go after those troops. One of the outcroppings was called the Pirate's Den. They said, "Johnson, go burn out those caves."

So, I said, "Okay." You know, you don't say no. So I sidle up alongside of a cave and I couldn't get the darn thing to work. You've got two triggers. A trigger at the front and you pull that and that starts the igniter, so there is flame going through there. The second trigger releases the napalm to go through the tube, past the igniter, and into the caves and at the Japanese and so on. I couldn't get the igniter to work. So I ran back and I said, "Hey, does anybody know how to make this damn thing work?"

They finally got the thing to work. It was rusty or something. Then they said, "Okay, go back and burn out those caves." I went back and I burned out three caves. And you have to be very careful not to have it splash back on you because you can burn yourself. So, that took care of the snipers in that Pirate's Den. There was no more shooting from it. And from what I can read, that's not a good way to die because you either get burned up or the oxygen is exhausted and you suffocate. So apparently, that's what happened to the Japanese in the Pirate's Den there.

That turned out to be the only time Wendell would use the flame-thrower.

We had a so-called surprise dawn attack on Kakazu Ridge. Well, I don't know what went wrong, but it was far after dawn when we attacked. Now, when you're carrying the flame-thrower in the company, you're the last guy. There are 170 or 180 guys ahead of you. And in this situation, the attack went down a steep hill and then up the steep other side and the Japanese were on the other side. The platoon sergeant was with me and by the time we got there, to the top of the hill to go down after the rest of the company had done it, the Japanese were all awake and they were firing machine guns and mortars and rifles and so on. And we said, this doesn't sound like a good idea to do. In our company, we lost something like sixty men that day from that attack. So the sergeant and I stayed up at the top, thinking discretion is the better part of valor or he who fights today and runs away, lives to fight another day.

I took the flame-thrower off and I had a rock on one side and the flame-thrower on the other as sort of protection. And the Japanese saw us and were sniping at us and mortaring us and so on, and one mortar shell landed on the other side of the flame-thrower and blew out the tanks – blew out the napalm tanks. But fortunately, it didn't explode. It didn't burn or anything. About twenty feet behind us, we noticed there was a circular hole and where we were was clearly not good because they could see us and they were firing at us. So we said, "one-two-three" and dashed back and jumped into the hole and got there without getting wounded. And we had to stay there all day long because whenever we raised our head to see what was going on – Zip! So we didn't get out of there till nighttime when it was too dark for them to shoot us. The battalion took serious losses in that first major battle.

And that's how I lost the flame-thrower.

Wendell Johnson describes the fighting on Okinawa as a 'meat grinder operation.'

And they had all the hills strongly fortified. Strongly meaning they had tunnels going from one side to the other side. Most of the time we'd get heavy fire from Japanese machine guns, rifles, mortars, and so on, we'd never see them because they were hidden in the tunnels. It wasn't until the flame-thrower tanks came along and would burn off the hillside that we could really see where the fire was coming from. But in the first part of that campaign, you just couldn't see where the Japanese were and so we took very heavy casualties. So we just kept grinding away and grinding away and grinding away and grinding away.

One thing about the infantry – stick around long enough and you'll get a promotion.

I was about halfway through the campaign and they made me platoon sergeant. In the infantry, if you survive, you advance. And out of 180 who landed, maybe 15 or 20 were still there. So I was one of the survivors and I guess that's how I got to be a platoon sergeant. But here I am, a twenty-one-year-old, and in charge of 20, 30, 40, eighteen-, nineteen-, twenty-year-olds, who are fresh off the boat. With those heavy casualties, you just get green young men and that's a real challenge when you think about it.

Many soldiers collected souvenirs on the battlefield, but it could be a dangerous hobby.

I was never a souvenir collector. Well, a little bit. But I didn't go into caves, for example, because that could be dangerous to your health because there could still be Japanese in there and we did lose some.

On Okinawa, there were some entrepreneurs who had pliers and there were many hillside tombs. These were concrete tombs with a little courtyard out in front of them. The Japanese would use them. They had machine guns in those and they would fire at us. You're not supposed to desecrate the tombs of the Okinawan natives, but hell, the Japanese are shooting at you from them. They were just like a pillbox. There were hundreds of these tombs on the hillsides. I did go and look at some of them and they had a system where they'd put grandma in a jar on the lowest shelf until grandma was reduced to bones and then they put her in a smaller jar up on the second shelf. And then when she was reduced to dust, they'd put her in an even smaller jar up on the top shelf. Well, the Japanese had a lot of gold teeth and some of our enterprising infantrymen would go in and pull out grandma's gold teeth and take the gold home. I never did that. Or they'd go in after maybe Japanese pistols or swords or something and I didn't do that, either.

Thousands of civilians on Okinawa were caught in the middle of the fierce fighting.

It was not unusual for villages to be burning when we went through them. The artillery would maybe set them on fire and so on. And one scene I remember particularly was a village we went through and here was this pond – a pretty sizable pond – and there's a woman out in the middle of it, very badly burned. She was in the water to reduce the burning sensation and she kept motioning her hands toward herself, which I think meant 'shoot me.' And well, what do you do? You're not a medic. You're not going to shoot her. It's against our code to do that kind of thing. So, I tried to find a medic to help take care of her and finally, we did get one to help her. But we're not going to shoot her. But here's a dramatic moment and how do you cope with that?

It took nearly three months to secure Okinawa. It would have been a miracle for an infantryman to survive the entire campaign without a scratch. Johnson knew his days were numbered.

We overran a lot of the Japanese. They would hide in caves and then at night, they'd come out of the caves and try to go through our lines back to their lines. Well, here we are on this pretty steep escarpment. It's called the Yayu Daki Escarpment. This had been the line for the Japanese for several days and we were perched halfway up this escarpment. It was like midnight and our troops had been coming up and down this trail all night long and here comes another group of a half-dozen smelly soldiers. We were all smelly, but I don't know who smelled worse – us or the Japanese. But anyhow, we found out that these were Japanese coming from behind our lines, trying to go through our lines to where the Japanese in front of our lines were. And so we got into a firefight at about midnight and we were throwing hand grenades and firing at them. We killed most of them and blocked them. Well anyhow, I think a bullet hit the rock against which I was leaning and splattered my back with metal and coral rock fragments. It wasn't that serious. I didn't go back right away or anything like that. I stayed another day, but it started to get infected and was starting to be bothersome so they said, "Hey Johnson, go on back and get it treated." So that's how I dropped out. It was not a serious wound, but it took a lot of attention. I probably had thirty, forty fragments in my back.

So I went back to the field hospital and they said, "Well, you need more attention. You need more glasses. You've got ringworm. And you've got hookworm." So they put me on a hospital ship back to Saipan.

After he recovered, Wendell was asked if he would like to transfer out of the infantry.

I was in the replacement depot there on Saipan and there was a 1ˢᵗ sergeant in an anti-aircraft ordnance battalion on the shores of Saipan who had enough points to go back, so they needed a replacement. I could be a replacement for him and they asked if I would like to do that. Would I like to get out of the infantry? Now, the rest of the division was on Mindoro (in the Philippines) *– what was left of it, anyway. They were getting ready to attack Japan. And I thought, well, maybe I've done my bit with* *first-wave landings in the Philippines and Okinawa. So I said, "Yeah, sure." I'd do it.*

When the war ended, men were sent home according to a point system.

I think I got to 54 points and I was there. And so in early December of '45, I found myself on a ship going back to the States. Now, these liberty ships take forever to get anywhere and it was like three weeks on the ship. But I finally got to the Chicago area and was discharged on December 29, 1945. And my folks had driven down from Muskegon, Michigan, which is a couple of hundred miles north of there, and we had a party. That's a happy memory. We stayed overnight at a nice hotel. It was like a New Year's Eve party, a pre-New Year's Eve party. So that was a happy ending to that situation.

Courtesy of Anthony Adams

I had to go to New York City. That was the closest recruiting office. It was in Grand Central Station. If you've ever been there, there's a great big concourse where all the people from the Long Island Railroad come running down the steps. Well, underneath the steps was a recruiting office. I went in and I told him I was going to enlist, which meant that I could pick my service. I could pick, supposedly, anything I wanted. The guy says, "Fine." I started through the line and he says, "Well, what do you want?"

I said, "Well, my brother is in the field artillery. I want the field artillery." I got to the end of the line and some guy had a bunch of rubber stamps in front of him, bang: U.S. Army Air Force – unassigned. I said I didn't want the Air Force.

He said, "Oh yeah, today's Air Force day." He said, "You'll like it. Don't worry about it."

Anthony A. Adams
U.S. Army Air Force

Tony Adams was inducted into the Army Air Force in November of 1942. After basic training, he attended radar school. He became a radar operator and was assigned to a bomber crew. His crew was sent to Hays, Kansas to train on a B-29.

We knew we had an airplane that was capable of going thirty-two hundred miles or more, but we didn't know if we were going to Europe, Asia, wherever. But they used to fly missions, simulated missions, from Hays, Kansas – Walker Field – to Cuba, or to New York City or to Montreal. And these were all round-trip, no landing. Hays was dry at that time. It wasn't Prohibition, but it was dry. So once in awhile, we used to fly booze missions to Chicago, Minneapolis....

Late in 1944, they got their orders to head overseas. Their destination was the Pacific island of Saipan.

Saipan was what they call 'secured,' but it really wasn't secured when we got there. We had these outdoor theaters and ours was called 'Surfside.' It looked across toward Tinian. And one time I was sitting there at the movies with some guy sitting next to me and he says, "Hey, Yank." I turn and it was a Jap from up in the hills.

Japanese soldiers were still hiding in the caves on Saipan. Patrols were sent out to flush out the stragglers. The Marines would often pick up souvenirs on these patrols, and occasionally they would offer to make a trade with the new flyboys on the island.

The Marines came back and they knew we had booze because of our officers getting it and if they didn't drink it, they'd give us some. So we would trade booze for souvenirs.

A Marine came down one day – a nice kid from Kansas, I believe – and he said, "I got a Japanese flag. What's it worth?"

I said, "Well, it's worth a bottle of Cutty Sark." So I gave him a bottle of Cutty Sark and he gave me a Japanese flag. He took off back to the hills to his base and we were inspecting the Japanese flag and right down in one corner it says: 'Property of the U.S. Army Air Force.' It was part of a parachute.

Adams was assigned to the 882nd Squadron, 500th Bomb Group, 73rd Wing, in the 20th Air Force. His crew named their B-29 'The Constant Nymph.' They flew their first mission on December 24, 1944.

You went up there the first time and you were scared. There was no doubt about it. The second time you were a little bit less than scared. The third time you got to thinking about the booze and stuff that you left behind in your locker.

We had a tradition if a guy was going on a mission and another crew had flown the day before and they weren't going, you left all your personal belongings with your buddy on the other crew. If you had booze and you didn't come back, they were to have a wake. It was common procedure.

At that point in the war in the Pacific, the bombers had to go it alone.

The first part, in December and in January and February of '45, none of us expected to come back from any mission that we went on because we realized that, hey, we don't have fighter escort. We're on our own and it's up to our gunners. But the gunners couldn't do anything about the anti-aircraft. The Japanese were real good on anti-aircraft up to about 15,000.

When General Curtis Lemay took over the command, the tactics for the 500th Bomb Group changed. The general ordered them to bomb their targets from 7,000 feet or less. In addition to carrying demolition bombs, the bombers were using incendiary bombs that caused massive firestorms.

We were going in at 7,000 and it was about midnight. We were right over Kuri Naval Base, which was near Tokyo. It was Yokosuka, Yokohama, and Kuri...they were all the bases that were right on the Bay of Tokyo. And we were going right over there and I dropped the bombs. Anything over six-tenths coverage of clouds, you went radar. And of course, at night when you get a six-tenths coverage, you had to drop by radar. I dropped them by radar. The camera is clicking away. I went to close the bomb bay doors and there was a horrible smell. So the flight engineer goes down into the bomb bay. He found half a cow and enough lumber to build a small house went up into the bomb bay. What had happened is, you had these fires on the ground and it was pretty bad. You had thermal updraft and of course, when you got in the thermal updraft, right away, you got into the downdraft. After the updraft, came the downdraft and it probably dragged us down to maybe 4,000 feet or less. The captain was flying that airplane and he said he thought he was at 3,000, but he couldn't swear. He just had a chance to look at the gauge at one time and then pull back on the stick to get it up. And when the doors closed, it closed in all this debris and the cow.

It was as if the cow and the parts of the barn had been caught in a fiery cyclone.

Obviously, the bombers did not always hit what they were aiming at. To check their accuracy, B-29s were equipped with cameras.

You couldn't lie because the minute you opened your bomb bay doors, you had a camera and it automatically started when the bombs dropped. As soon as the bombs were released, the camera would start. It wouldn't stop until the door switch was activated to close the bomb bay door. So, if you tried to lie, you were caught.

On one mission, that camera almost led to a court-martial for Tony's crew.

They accused us of dropping a bomb inside the Emperor's palace. It had a moat affair around it with a wall. At the time, Hirohito supposedly wanted to stop, or didn't want the war. Tojo, Yamamoto, and a couple other guys, supposedly, talked him out of it and convinced him that he was doing the right thing. Our intelligence theory was, stay away from the palace. Well, what happened was, we were on a fire raid and we got a guy overhead of us and we pulled evasion tactics to get away from him and in the process we went directly over the palace. The camera was operating and they didn't know if it was our bombs or not, but somebody's bombs hit the ball field inside the palace grounds.

After several firebombing missions, Adams had to take a break.

I had to take a one-month R and R because after you sit up there and you look down on sixty-five square miles of city burning, you kind of get guilty. You know it's the enemy, but still, they're civilians. But the only reason we bombed Tokyo so much was because the Japanese system was, every family had to do something for the war effort. Every family had their own little factory. They would make parts for gun sights, for bomb sights, for airplane parts, in each house and that stuff was all collected and sent to the factory.

Their biggest factory was a Mitsubishi Aircraft Factory, which was in Hamamatsu. Originally, back – oh, a thousand years ago – they made fiddles and these lutes and stuff that the old Japanese used to play – the Kabuki dancers and that. Well, the fiddle factory was turned into the Mitsubishi Aircraft Factory and we always called it the fiddle factory when we were going on that raid. Most of the material there came from individual houses in Tokyo.

You still felt guilty. I mean, from what we were told, it got so hot that it drove the people into Tokyo Bay and even the water close to shore would boil because you had about 300 B-29s on one raid and they're all dropping firebombs, plus demolition bombs. It could make a pretty good size fire.

B-29 missions often lasted more than fourteen hours. To save fuel, the men in charge decided to lighten the loads on the bombers.

I didn't know until after it was over that on some of these missions we had gunners on board, but no bullets. They would fly night missions, fire raid missions, with empty canisters. The gunners knew it, but they wouldn't tell us. They flew along as observers. And the reason for that is that our fuel had to be managed. On most trips you went on, you climbed to say 15,000 then you dropped down and then you climbed again and then you dropped down. And each time you climbed you were eating up fuel, so they would take as much weight off of the airplanes as they possibly could. And on nighttime missions, they figured the Japanese fighters weren't that prevalent.

Even with these fuel-saving measures, there was barely enough fuel for these lengthy missions. If there were any problems, the bombers might not make it safely back to their base. On a mission in February of '45, Tony's plane had a problem.

On February 25, 1945 we were on a Tokyo raid and we got up over the South China Sea and the weather was really bad. It was like the Cedar Point ride, Demon Drop. We came back, went to circle the field, dropped the gear and nothing happened. We didn't have enough fuel to go around a second time, so the skipper said let's crank the gear down by hand. Well, this took fifteen minutes and it was a hard crank. It was like an old Model T Ford. We didn't have that time. So he decided he was just going to take it in and crash-land it. We didn't have seat belts then. Well, the gunners did, but I didn't have one. I was on a swivel chair and I could butt myself up against the radar table and I had my chest chute and that would hold me steady. So I was braced up against that and I sat sideways facing the star (painted on the outside of the plane). The skipper told me to lower the antenna as far as it will go. He couldn't hear it scrape up front, so he said, "When you hear that thing scrape, you holler out." So when I heard it scrape, I hollered out. He eased it and then when he got it going slow enough, down to about sixty or seventy miles an hour, it settled down. There wasn't anything we could do then, but just slide. It bent the propellers. It curled them up real good. We all got out okay. I rammed my nose against, I guess it must have been the scope, and I wound up with a deviated septum. But we all got out of the airplane and everybody lit up a cigarette, like idiots. We were like a hundred feet away from it, but it never caught fire.

The crew survived. They were lucky, but not as lucky as 'The Constant Nymph.'

So they took the airplane and they put gear pins in it to keep the gear down and flew it to Guam. They disassembled it, put it on a boat and shipped it over to the United States and took it around the country to sell war bonds – the fuselage. So the airplane did serve some good.

During the final years of the war, the Japanese Air Force began using a desperate tactic – suicide bombers.

At nighttime, the Japs used to use what they called the 'Baka' bomb. It was a V-2 rocket with a kamikaze pilot in it. And he would try to ram the lead aircraft, if he came upon a formation. And in formation, you flew wingtip to wingtip and there wasn't much room for error.

On one mission, we were missed by about two or three hundred feet by a kamikaze pilot. The tail gunner got him. He missed us and he was heading for an airplane just below us and the tail gunner happened to spot him and he got him with the twenty-millimeter cannons. Luckily, he had shells in the twenty-millimeters that time.

When Adams landed on Saipan, his tour of duty was supposed to be twenty-five missions. After he reached number twenty-five, he had a meeting with his commander, General Lemay.

They flew me down to Guam and I went into the commander's office and he was sitting there and he said, "Well, sergeant, you got twenty-five missions? I said twenty-five was tops, right?"

I said, "Yes."

He said, "Well, we increased it to thirty. But if you're really burned out…" –

blah-blah-blah-blah.

> *So I said, "No, okay. I'll go to thirty."*

After Tony flew mission number thirty, he had another meeting with the general.

> *At thirty, I was called down again and I was told, you could stay on and we'll think about sending you to O.C.S. – Officers' Candidate School. I thought about it and I said I'd stay on, but I will not go over thirty-five.*

He ended up flying a total of thirty-three missions.

> *The last mission, I think it was to – I don't know if it was Oda or Yokohama – but it was almost my **last** mission. We ran into real heavy flak. Luckily, I was sitting on my swivel chair and I had three or four flak curtains. They were pieces of fabric that had steel woven into them – steel strips woven into them. And they would have some give and what we used to do was set them up around our back and behind because the star was back there and the guy was aiming at the star* (on the outside of the plane). *I was sitting on two of them.*

Their target that day was a battleship in a navy yard.

> *The battleship was firing at us. We got a close hit. It was actually a near miss, but the fragments came up and came through the floor. It got the radar antenna and came up and got through the seat and into the flak curtains. When we got back from that mission, there were quite a few holes in that airplane. We came back and I went into the dispensary and I had a few scratches. And they asked me what had happened and I said, "Well, I got hit in the butt by a battleship."*

Adams' war was over. But after all he had seen – even from more than a mile in the air – he couldn't forget.

> *Well, it was nightmares. My aunt tells me this. I don't know anything about it. But I had the attic room and she'd hear me and she'd come up and I'd be hanging on the bedpost. Going through missions is what I was doing. That was, oh, four or five months.*

Most veterans of the Second World War believe if the atomic bombs had not been dropped, the Japanese would not have surrendered. Tony Adams was there. He has a different opinion.

> *The results in the Pacific mostly were due to the firebombs. I don't care what*

anybody says about the atomic bomb. We had them beat. There was no doubt about it. After our fire raids, they were ready to scream 'uncle.' The atomic bomb was just an exclamation point. That was all.

GI Christmas card
Courtesy of Bernie Swope

Then of course, D-Day came along and we knew it was coming because they painted those black and white stripes on the plane the day before and we were stood down. We didn't fly. And we had inklings, too. I'll never forget Axis Sally used to broadcast to us and it was a lot of fun to listen to her because we had high morale and she didn't affect us. But she had a little theme song when it got near D-Day. It was sung to the tune of The Camels Are Coming: "D-Day is coming. We're waiting for you."

Jack R. Barensfeld
U.S. Army Air Force

When Jack Barensfeld joined the Army Air Force in 1943, he was hoping to become a pilot. After he completed his flight training, he anxiously awaited his assignment.

Then in the early darkness before breakfast, they'd call you out to a formation in front of the barracks and they would announce the classification of the various fliers as they came up. You'd stand there and they'd say, 'Jones, J.W., navigator. Albright, A., bombardier, etc.'... then, 'J.R. Barensfeld, pilot.'

Jack got his wish and began training to become a fighter pilot. He was sent to Great Britain in March of 1944. There was more training and then the new arrivals were asked to pick their outfits.

The 9ᵗʰ Air Force was just forming, getting ready for D-Day. It had come up from the Middle East. They were at Atcham. I later heard it referred to as 'Clobber College.' The instructor there, Billy King, sold us a bill of goods and said, "Come on down with me. We're on the East Coast, between London and Calais, France and it's very primitive, but we get the action. You could go to the 8ᵗʰ Air Force and fly escort and be bored to death, but down in our outfit, the 9ᵗʰ Air Force, we fly close support – dive-bombing and strafing." I'll never forget, his expression was 'chasing the Krauts out of the weeds.' That's the way he put it. And so seventeen of us, who had come over together and who had trained together, went with Billy.

Barensfeld joined the 362ⁿᵈ Fighter Group and in a matter of days, he flew his first combat mission. He was not afraid for his own safety on that first flight.

I didn't have the slightest fear. The only fear I had was that I would screw up and I would embarrass myself and I wouldn't match up to the trained, experienced fighter pilots. I wanted more than anything in the world to be accepted and to measure up. That was my fear – that I would make a mistake, not that I would get shot at.

But Jack knew if he was going to survive, he'd need a little help.

People ask me if I prayed. Yes, I prayed. I think everybody did. When you're

107

sitting there in your cockpit, waiting for start engine times, it was quiet. Then you'd see a flare go up from the control van and that meant start engines and you would taxi out. But when I was sitting there waiting for start engines, I would pray. But I felt it would be hypocritical to ask God to protect me on a mission, especially because there was a German pilot not very far away praying to the same God. So I always said, "Dear God, I hope you see fit to bring me back." And He did. Time after time, He did.

On June 5, 1944, the pilots were briefed on the next day's mission. They had attacked targets in France many times before, but this time it would be different. They would be flying air support for 'Operation Overlord,' D-Day.

We walked back from that briefing and we were all thrilled because we had been waiting for this. I was walking with Bobby Berger, one of my buddy pilots. I said, "Boy, tomorrow we get a chance to make a name for ourselves. That's what the Germans have been waiting for. We're going to be over there and the sky's going to be full of German planes." We hadn't seen that many because the Germans had been pretty much beaten down by that time – in the air. And Bobby Berger said, "Jack, I'll bet you a five-pound note." At that time it was twenty bucks. "I'll bet you a five-pound note that we don't see any Germans."

I said, "You're crazy. That's what they're waiting for." I said, "You're on."

Barensfeld's mission on D-Day began with a frightening sight.

There were several planes ahead of us that were scheduled to take off first. One of them couldn't get enough power and he went off the end of the runway and burst into flames. And I'll never forget you could see the reflection of the flames glow against the clouds. The clouds maybe were a couple thousand feet. But that was quite a traumatic thing to take off over. But it turned out that the pilot survived. We were flying P-47 Thunderbolts and that good old rugged Thunderbolt held together and the pilot had time to jump out of the plane and run away and he wasn't even scratched. We didn't know that at the time, of course. We found that out when we got back.

Our job on D-Day was to escort C-47 transport planes towing gliders to reinforce the paratroops that had landed the night before.

The glider landings on D-Day were a near disaster.

We were over there off the Cherbourg Peninsula and the C-47s turned off the English Channel to go over land and then they got shot at plenty. The German flak gunners had a lot of experience by that time and they were pretty good. We saw quite a few of them get hit. Then they started to release the gliders and it was a very, very bad experience because a lot of the gliders were hit in the air and they would make a tight circle and land in those damn hedgerows. And the fields weren't big enough and the gliders would split open when they hit and you'd see troops and even small artillery pieces bounding out of the things. And I thought to myself, 'Boy, if they're relying on this mission for the success of D-Day, we're in trouble.'

As they flew back to England, some of those doubts about D-Day began to fade.

When we got over the water, our ships were strewn out in front of us. You could walk on our ships all the way back to England, practically. Our battleships were offshore, shooting inland to Normandy. And it was something to see those big guns on those battleships and the huge flame that would shoot out and the smoke and then the shock wave on the water.

Barensfeld's squadron returned to the field and waited, and Jack lost a bet.

We came back and then were put on reserve for the rest of the day. We sat in the airplanes with the engines warmed up, but we weren't needed because I think the Germans put up two airplanes? That's what <u>The Longest Day</u> said. That's all. There was no resistance at all. And I lost my twenty bucks.

After the Allies established a beachhead, the 362nd Fighter Group moved to Normandy.

In those days, we were trying to keep the Germans from reinforcing the beachhead and as they would come up, we would catch them on the roads. If the weather was good and we were around, they would hide under any cover they could find. But by flying low and looking under the trees, you could see them. And we were especially pleased when we could find a fuel tank truck. You'd circle around and mark the place and come down and strafe the truck and it would burst into the most beautiful flames you ever saw. It was quite the thing. We used to think it was a lot of fun. Of course, they were shooting at us, too. But flying so low, you'd have a pretty good chance because you're only exposed for such a short time. Although, we had some nasty losses there – that's when I lost one of my buddies, Craig Gilbert. He was shot down right after D-Day by an enemy airplane. It was a fluke. Then we also lost Al

Bessie, a wonderful young man, very religious. The worst swear word I ever heard him say was not even a swear word. It was 'dang.' He was killed up near Cherbourg while strafing. Then it was just Roy Barker and myself left from the buddies I first trained with.

On July 25, 1944, Jack's squadron was ordered to bomb a bridge near Caen. Shortly after takeoff, his P-47 was hit by ground fire.

We flew over, evidently, a very high concentration of German forces, either an armored division coming up to reinforce the beachhead or something. Being low under the overcast, we were shot at. I could see the tracers coming. I could feel my plane getting hit. Red flashes. White flashes. When you were low and strafing, you could hear the guns shooting at you – those automatic weapons – even above your engine sound. It didn't scare us, but it was attention-getting. So I knew I was hit – that the plane was hit bad. My wingman, I don't know what happened to him. He was killed. I made a 180-degree turn, trying to get out of there and my plane was vibrating very bad and I could smell gasoline very strong. I knew I had to get somewhere. The plane kept vibrating and we were low. I didn't have that much space and I looked down and there was no place you could make a forced landing in those hedgerows. I thought, 'I'm going to have to bail out if this thing quits.' I was hoping to get out of this fire. They were still shooting at me, because I could see tracers. And the engine quit. And the easiest thing I ever did was get out of that airplane – no ifs, ands or buts. I knew I didn't have much time. Evidently, I had some forethought about this. I remembered my training. Unhook your oxygen mask and your radio stuff. Make sure your helmet is on and, of course, release your seatbelt and shoulder straps. Put your foot on the throttle, which was on the left side, and dive. Of course, the canopy was jettisoned as part of this routine. Then, I dove over the side and I got clear of the airplane. I knew I had to pull the ripcord – the d-ring we called it – soon because I was very low. I think I swung once, maybe twice, and hit the ground quite hard. It hurt. I thought, 'Boy, I hope I'm in friendly territory.' I didn't know. So I did the routine. You throw your 'Mae West' one way. You gather up your chute and you take off in a direction that you hope is right. By that time, you're so confused that you don't know whether you are going towards or away from the enemy. I was in quite a bit of pain from the way I hit the ground hard, but I went a few hundred yards and found a place to hide. I tried to hide the chute. That's a big job because that's a big twenty-four-foot canopy with all the shroud lines. I stayed there for about five or ten minutes, trying to get my thoughts together and wondering, 'Now what the hell do I do?' Then I hear voices and I thank God, they're English voices. They were coming from over the side of the hedgerow. I didn't see anybody, but I heard the voices. And I listened for one and made sure they were English and then I yelled out, "Hey! I'm a Yank pilot, shot down. I need help." Silence. Five minutes go by...ten minutes. What the heck? I said, "Hey!"

All of a sudden from behind me, "Put your hands up, buddy." It was Canadians. I landed near the Gold Beach section and they were Canadians that had been out for two weeks under combat conditions. They all had beards. They looked straggly and dirty with muddy uniforms. These guys weren't anything to fool with.

They weren't sure if Barensfeld was an American or a German spy in an American uniform. He was taken back to their HQ and interrogated.

An officer came up and recognized that I had an American flier's suit and then he said, "Where are you from?"

I said, "From Cleveland, Ohio."

He said, "Oh? I'm from Toronto." He said, "What's the tallest building in Cleveland?"

I said, "The Terminal Tower."

He said, "Okay."

They took Jack Barensfeld back to his squadron and his flight surgeon sent him to a field hospital.

I went to sleep that evening and slept right through till about ten o'clock the next morning. I didn't realize how tired I was and I felt much better and got wonderful care. And they found a blood patch on my flying suit, on my left thigh. I was hit by a fragment of something and they dug it out later on and brought it to me. It was a piece of my own airplane. It was an aluminum piece of my plane. It wasn't German. But that's the only wound I had, and then the injury to the back. So I stayed at the hospital there for a little more than two weeks and they gave me rest and therapy and obviously some muscle relaxant or something. But I always healed fast and by God, I said to the doctor, "I want to get back to my unit."

He said, "Oh no, we'll send you back to the States."

It never occurred to me that I could go back to the States and I didn't want to. All my buddies were back at my unit. I had a good start and I was getting along very well and I said, "No, no, I've got to get back to my unit."

He said, "Okay, whatever you say."

Jack could have been on his way home, but he chose to return to the fight. His squadron provided air support for the ground troops advancing across Europe.

And we always flew supporting General Patton and his Army. We were attached to him and when he would move forward, we would follow them. And we got to know his armored division units pretty well and it was a wonderful system.

On December 16, 1944, Barensfeld flew a mission on one of the most important days of the war.

I was lucky enough to fly one of the first missions on the first day of The Bulge. And as you know from history, after that first day, the weather closed in and we didn't fly for five or six days. It was just pea soup fog. We were very frustrated. But that first day, we had a mission of strafing a pontoon bridge across the Our River, which is on the border between Germany and Belgium. Of course, this was only a few hours after the attack started. There's been confusion there. It was said that there wasn't much air activity on that first day. That's wrong. There was all kinds of air activity. The Germans had all their airplanes up that day. They had been hoarding them for this big attack – The Battle of the Bulge – and it was quite a melee. When we got back to the field, we were always debriefed by our intelligence officer. I was now a squadron leader, after all these missions and he was interrogating me for his report, which was routine, and I said, "The Germans are crossing this pontoon bridge from east to west."

He said, "Jack, you mean from west to east, don't you?"

I said, "No." That's how complacent we were. After chasing the Germans all through France, we couldn't believe that they were turning back on us.

When the weather broke, the Army Air Force went to work.

Finally the weather cleared and for several days we had a real heyday up there. Beautiful weather and we'd catch these Germans out in the open. They would try to stay hidden, but sometimes they had to move because our ground troops had forced them to move. It was either move or get captured – so we would catch them out in the open and we had quite a great heyday there.

Near the end of December 1944, Jack finally got a break from combat.

At New Year's, I was allowed to go to Paris for four days' leave. A little R and R, we called it – rest and recuperation. Of course we enjoyed that very much. We had a little airplane that would fly us back and forth, so it was no trouble. But, when I got back from that in the first or second week in January, I was stunned because when I came back, one of my fellow pilots says, "Jack, Roy Barker bought the farm yesterday."

Jack's best buddies were the three pilots he met during training back in the States.

Well, he was the third one and we each had over a hundred missions and that was the one that hurt me the most because Roy and I had a deal that we wouldn't get clobbered separately.

I've got a picture taken at our final training base in Louisiana where there are the four of us in front of a P-47 and I am the only one of the four left.

It was hard not to think about his pals, but Barensfeld continued to fly.

I kept flying till the end of January and then the flight surgeon came back and when he heard that Roy had been killed, he had me grounded. He said, "Jack, you've had enough. You're going home."

Jack flew a total of 103 combat missions.

In February, I got on a ship and came back. There were only a few of us on this wonderful ship. The food was wonderful and we landed in New York Harbor and there was not a dry eye. It was quite a thing.

And Jack remembered that prayer.

"Dear God, I hope you see fit to bring me back."

Only seven of the seventeen pilots that joined the 362nd Fighter Group with Barensfeld came home.

But that's what I wanted to say to you is how fortunate I was. I just had that one scratch, one bailout, and to be so lucky to fly all that time and to get home safe and sound. It was really something.

We had to go up to the Sandusky area. There was a place up there for our physicals. And we had to go through the business, which we did. There were two other women from Lutheran along with me. And I remember my mother saying, yes, fine, I could join the Army, but she didn't want me leaving the States.

So I very naively told the sergeant, "I want to join, but I can't leave the United States of America."

And he looked at me and he said, "You will be in the Army, ma'am. We give the orders. You don't."

Jeanne Lucas Hacker
U.S. Army Nurse Corps

When America went to war, Jeanne Hacker was working as a nurse in Cleveland, Ohio. After she turned twenty-one, she decided to enlist. She reported for induction in the summer of 1943 and was assigned to the 38th Field Hospital and sent to Camp Campbell, Kentucky. At Camp Campbell, the nurse recruits got a taste of life in the Army.

Most of the time we were at Camp Campbell, we had basic training like the men. We had to learn to use a rifle and we had to shoot it. They said just in the event something happened, they wanted us to be able to pick it up and know what to do with it. We had to crawl on our bellies under barbed wire with live ammunition shooting. We had to climb the ropes and the ladders. I don't know how I did it, now that I think about it. We lost two or three of the women there. It was just too much physically for them. It was rough. And if we weren't doing that kind of thing, we were marching – with or without packs. They were trying to say you could go anywhere. You could be in a bad unit. You could be in the city and do nothing, but you have to be ready.

In December of 1943, the 38th shipped out. They were sent to Hawaii for more tough, physical training, but Jeanne got a little break from that when she was selected for surgical training.

I was fortunate. I got out of about a week of it because they took me and I spent about four or five days at Schofield and about four or five days at Tripler. I remember the Schofield Navy doctor so well because he was so nice. He was an orthopedic doctor. I told him I don't know anything about amputations. He said, "Well my dear, you're going to have to learn because that's what you're going to be running into." And we really worked on linen packs and the surgical packs. The instruments that were needed for amputations and all that kind of stuff like gunshot wounds. And I had all that special training. I didn't work on things like appendectomies and hemorrhoidectomies and hysterectomies – all that crap. It was strictly the stuff that the Army would use.

As part of their indoctrination for the move to a combat zone, the men and women of the 38th were shown a series of informational films.

They were telling about what you did if you were captured. All you did was: 'N-767501.' I'll never forget my number – my A.N.C. number. It comes to me before Social Security or anything. You gave your name, rank and serial number and nothing else. And we'd see horrible movies of people being tortured and whatever. They'd take women away and they'd be screaming and you could imagine what was next. But then, they showed these movies about this area where we'd be going and they'd have a lot of typhoons. And they had these beautiful palm trees and they'd show palm trees waving down to the ground. And it showed these natives and they'd go way up high and they would have this big rope and they'd slap it around the tree and they'd slap it around themselves. Then they'd be on the tree and the thing would go down like this and hit the ground. All of us sat there and nobody said anything, including the fellas. When it got through, somebody said, "We're supposed to do that?" Everybody just started laughing like mad.

Yes, according to the instructions in the movie, the best way to survive a tropical storm was to lash yourself to a palm tree. But, when the 38th landed on Kwajalein in May of 1944, they had a pleasant surprise.

And when we landed on the island of Kwajalein, there was not one tree, not one blade of grass, nothing left. And our one nurse, who was quite a character, says, "Oh, thank God. There aren't any trees to worry about." I'll never forget that. Everybody just roared because we were all thinking of that movie and wondering what would happen.

The nurses were taken to their quarters and after their long journey all they wanted was a nice refreshing shower.

We were all thinking it's going to feel so good to get a shower. We were so dirty. We drove in these jeeps and got to our barracks. We were filthy. We looked like raccoons. Our head nurse said, "Now ladies, you can take showers, but I just want to tell you that they will be cold saltwater. I brought some special soap that will make it easier for lathering." We just died. And the whole time we were down there, we had cold saltwater showers. But at least you showered and you got the stuff off and then you took the towel and wiped the salt off. That was your shower. But you can live through anything if you have to. We managed.

The island of Kwajalein had been secured, but reminders of the battle remained.

Somebody said to me later, you probably went swimming. But we didn't because there were bodies still floating up out of the water from the Kwajalein battle. Most of them were Japanese, but occasionally you'd get an American, which was sad.

And when we first got there, the stench was so bad and we found out it was the bunkers. They had built these bunkers all over and they wouldn't come out. They'd just shoot at our guys.

So eventually, they'd throw grenades in the holes and that would be the end of them. Then you had to wait a while. And after we were there, they spent a lot of time cleaning out the bunkers and the smell got better. But as long as there were a couple in the bunkers, you had that smell that just hung over everything.

The new arrivals were taken to the 38th Field Hospital.

They took us over there to show us what was what. The men were in tents and we had a Quonset hut for our surgery. We had four operating room tables and when we were busy and a bunch of men flew in, you had them all busy at once.

Our corpsmen were very well trained. They were very good at scrubbing and things like that. In time, we taught them how to do the shots. They did a lot of the inter-muscular shots, but I remember they were very fussy about the morphine. They never wanted it to go in the wrong hands and get waylaid. Occasionally, I guess, some would disappear and they wondered about it, so the nurses were more or less responsible for the morphine shots.

In the beginning, casualties were light and everyone had a chance to try to prepare for what was coming.

The first couple days we were there it was pretty good, which was fine because it gave us a chance to get the feel. And then they started coming in. They air-evacuated them in – you'd get thirty or forty at a clip. They'd put them on hammock-type things in the planes.

It was kind of rough because you had to try to decide who was the most crucial that you could help and save. And there were ones that you would just try to put them out of their agony. You could tell with their internal injuries they weren't going to make it anyhow, so why amputate and put them through other stuff. It was a very hard decision because they were all so young and vital, you know. It was just sad. It just made me sick.

Jeanne would often work twelve-hour days. When she did get a break, she would occasionally try to fill that time by writing a letter to her family. But what exactly could she write about?

They were so boring. They would say 'it's another hot day.' And it was hot, extremely hot on Kwajalein. You'd be laying there and there would be water dripping off. And in surgery, we'd be going around as a circulating nurse wiping the foreheads of the people working because they were just constantly wet.

But in the letters, you couldn't say that we were in the central Pacific or anything. The first two or three letters came back to me practically cut out. I had censor's marks all over them. They went through them and you weren't to tell anybody what you were doing. They knew I was in a hospital. I said we were in this small hospital and I said there are not many nurses, that kind of thing.

Jeanne remembers one day when she was working triage, helping to decide which of the wounded had a chance to survive. A young soldier had wounds that were usually fatal, but Jeanne thought if they operated, he just might make it.

We were deciding and they said they were going to give up on this one kid. He had been hit in the stomach and they thought his internal injuries were too bad. I said, "What do we have to lose?" We took him in and he lived, which was so good. It made me feel good for days, months, years. And later on, he was ready to go back to the States and he had heard about me. Somebody told him that I helped to save his life. I talked to him and he was crying and I was crying. And I wish I had gotten his name. I think back on so many of them and think, oh, I hope he made it. He seemed to be good when he left, but you never know. I've thought of him so many times.

Jeanne Hacker remembers the men who made it and of course, she remembers those who didn't.

Then I think of this other one who was supposed to be so good and we went in one day and he just quietly died and I felt bad because I thought he really had a chance. And he had just gotten married and his wife was pregnant when all this started. I think of him so much because he just quietly slept his life away, which is the way to go, I guess. And we didn't have time for autopsies, so he probably had internal bleeding that was missed. I'm sure that's what happened.

> *It was horrible when they died when you had them on the table. You'd think they were going to be all right, but then that would be it. And you know, those days you didn't take the time. You couldn't do all the resuscitation. You didn't have the whole blood. You didn't have the facilities that you have now. We couldn't have saved them and they would have needed constant care that we couldn't have given them. You didn't have room for them. We had no intensive care units. And you think now, a lot of them would have been saved.*

It's not surprising that there were times when Jeanne would need to somehow escape all this.

> *I was on call basically all the time and one night not too long after we were there, I was feeling just a little depressed and everything. We had this little gathering and I had a couple of beers and a shot for a chaser. And oh, I was feeling good, so I went to bed. About two hours after I was in bed, we get the call. Out you went. I can still remember this as vivid as yesterday. We did twelve to fourteen hours of working nonstop and I was just dry-heaving. Every chance I'd get, I would go out because I was so miserable. And this corpsman, Reby, was so great. He was a master sergeant and he knew more than most of the doctors, a lot of the new ones anyhow. He came out and was holding my head and saying, 'Oh, just stick with it.' He was so good. But it kind of put me off drinking for a long, long time.*

When the Navy came to Kwajalein, it was good times and good food.

> *They would eat high on the hog, as they used to say themselves. That was their expression. They got oranges and they got Spam. People complain about Spam, but we were thrilled to death to get Spam. And there were these two fliers that we got quite acquainted with, Melba and I. They had a short shelf life. I wonder what happened to them. I'm afraid they might have been killed even before we left down there. They would come over and one of them would have a can of Spam and the other one would have an orange. So we would take it and divide it. Can you imagine cutting a can of spam into eighteen pieces? And we'd take the oranges and cut them. It would be hysterical. We had more fun doing it, making sure they were equal. And every time they'd come, they'd say we know better than to come over here without having any stuff to offer.*

The Navy boys were certainly willing to share their food, but they did want a little something in return.

But then they got so that they'd ask us to eat, but we always had to have two or three of us in a group, never alone. So I said, "Okay, we'd like to come to eat, but we have to bring friends with us. I have to bring two women with me."

"Why?"

"Because I just can't go off with you alone." And then Melba would do the same thing. So we'd end up with about six of us. They were around every week and we rotated and all the nurses got a chance to eat. And we'd eat in the room with the Navy big shots and oh, it was fun. They were all dressed up and we were as dressed up as we could be.

I just saw this movie, <u>Mister Roberts</u> not long ago and I said to my husband when it started, 'What he is trying to make happen here, won't happen. I've been there.' So anyway, they were always trying to get one of us off and we had more fun. We knew what they were doing and they knew that we knew what they were doing and it was a fun experience. And they would always make sure that we had a couple of oranges and Spam to take back with us. They just had fun meeting and talking to women and having an experience other than just what they were doing all the time.

For the most part, the ladies on Kwajalein behaved themselves. But one nurse did get into a little trouble, and back in the '40s her trouble was considered scandalous.

One of our nurses managed to get pregnant toward the very end and she was a favorite of our head nurse, who would go with her to the colonel's place. Our head nurse and her and the colonel had a major or whatever. And she got pregnant. It was funny, she was there and all at once, one day she was gone. Everybody said, 'Where's Tindell? Where's Tindell?' Then later on it filtered back, which was too bad. I always felt bad about it because she was kind of a sitting duck.

In February of 1945, the 38th began receiving casualties from Iwo Jima.

Iwo Jima was so bad. They had a lot of deaths and they would ship them home for burial and the ships would stop at Kwajalein. They used the ships for that and they would take the long-term patients that they thought they could manage. And they would be filled and they would stop and drop off some of the wounded and pick up some of our people, but they didn't have much room because they had so many bodies.

It was just terrible.

One of the wounded dropped off at the hospital was a high-ranking Japanese naval officer.

And our men just got so furious. They said why do we have to take care of him and they'd go on and on. And he acted like he didn't understand a word of English the whole time he was there. He was so inscrutable. Their faces just don't give a thing away. He was there quite a while because they said they want him alive. They wanted to ship him back to Washington as soon as they can get him there. He had pretty serious injuries to start with, so they had to keep him there and people flew in to talk to him.

The day he was leaving I was on night duty and that morning, he said he wanted to talk to the nurse. So I went up to him and he says, "Thank you, Lieutenant Lucas, for excellent service given." In perfect English. And then he smiled. He actually smiled because all of our faces were just struck dumb. And the rumor afterward was that he had been educated in the States. He was taking everything in that was going on around, you know. He heard about all the horrible Japs and what they do. I used to say to this one guy who was determined he was going to do away with him, I said, "Listen, I know exactly who will be responsible if something happens to him." And we realized it was serious and we couldn't let anything happen to him. Not on our shift, anyway.

But that was fascinating to me. I'll never forget him. He just absolutely had no look whatsoever, just completely blank like he just didn't know what was happening all around him and he wasn't missing a trick.

In August of 1945 the war ended, but the job for the 38th Field Hospital continued.

August 6th, I think, the bomb was dropped on Japan. It was Janet's – one of the nurses' – birthday. And everybody started yelling and screaming. I was in my quarters and I heard all these people yell and scream all over the place. Then I found out what had happened and why everybody was so thrilled. But then we stayed on nearly four months after that because we had men coming through yet. So we stayed there until around the 1st of December.

Jeanne Hacker was discharged from the U.S. Army on January 17, 1946.

If you don't think too much about it, sometimes it seems like it never happened or it was a fun experience. But then when you think about it, you realize that it wasn't that much fun for anybody, really. This whole war thing is so stupid because it never cures anything. Never. It just makes you lose a lot of good people – a lot of good men – that should go on to a better life.

A Letter from the Battlefield

Nov. 21, 1944

Dear Friend,

Here's a paragraph that I wrote after one of the toughest spots I'd been in, which should give you a good idea of how I feel about all this, and something I think everyone at home should know.

The papers & magazines glorify the heroes of the war. But who can tell the story of the wounded man who has done his best and payed the price for his efforts. While the battle rages, he must lay there, helpless, unable to move, hoping and praying that help will come before it's too late. And when it does come, each minute seems like an eternity, the agonizing pain of being moved, the shells landing closer & closer. Fear, pain & shock surround him. Yet he smiles when you bandage him, and regardless of how hard and trying the trip back is, with each sudden jerk, like a knife, and each step we take is only a blurred dull pain, he never complains. Gratefully he acknowledges the proffered cigarette, or a drink of water, and when we are finally safe from danger, he thanks you humbly and says, "Gee, I'm sorry I was so much trouble to you." Can one forget these things? Will it ever be possible for him to tell you the thousand things he thought of as he waited in a living hell, and death stared him in the face? These are stories that are never told, but that happen to someone somewhere in No Man's Land. If you'd ever walk through it, you'd understand why it's called that, and especially so in the black of the night. I know of nothing that is more terrifying than that, when your own footsteps, and the crackle of the twigs you step on are noises that are magnified to the utmost, and the shriek of the cold wind, like the sound of a shell whistling through the air at you, and the shadows of the trees loom as enemy soldiers staring at you with a pointed gun. Then a sudden burst of light covers the sky, an enemy flare, and down you go, with your heart beating wildly, hoping you haven't been seen. I suppose I could go on and on, but all this answers nothing, and I wonder what it means to the rest of the world. I tell this to you, for I know that you too can feel all of this.

> *Yours Sincerely*
> *"Maurie"*

Courtesy of Maury Feren

I never got any training. All the training I got was in the field. I learned a lot on the field – what to do and tourniquets, whatever it might be. You learned real fast and you try to help people and people moan and cry 'Mother' and it's a terrible, terrible thing. Those words remain in your mind forever. You can hear people moaning for help, 'Doc! Doc!' It never leaves you because you know that there were people that you never got to.

Maury Feren

U. S. Army

Maury Feren was visiting with his mother on the day Pearl Harbor was attacked.

When we heard the news bulletin, my mother, who was an optimist, said, "You'll never go to the Army because you have a deviated septum and you don't breathe too good."

In addition to that, when the war began, Maury was married with a child.

Nobody in that period believed that they would take pre-Pearl Harbor fathers. And I was twenty-eight and I thought that was quite old for the Army, not knowing what they really were thinking.

In January of 1943, Feren received his draft notice and he had to leave his family and his business.

I had a big wholesale produce business. I just started the business and I was working very hard trying to get it going. That's a very demanding business because it's all perishable and it was a matter of trying to find my way in that business as an owner because I had worked for other people for many years.

He reported for basic training and began his life in the Army.

It was a very big adjustment because I had been an individual owner and ran my own business and never took orders; I was giving orders. That was difficult.

After Basic, Maury tried to get a transfer to the Quartermaster Corps.

I applied because I thought I had a good opportunity to do something really good. I thought I'd be great in quartermaster, but they didn't even listen to that and put me right into the infantry. I was put in an anti-tank group. Anti-tank groups have seven men behind the cannon. The jeep carries the cannon and each man has a position that they take so that when we have to get ready to shoot, that thing opens up and everybody has a particular job.

Feren was assigned to the 5th Division, 2nd Infantry Regiment. They shipped overseas to England late in the spring of 1944. About two weeks after D-Day, they crossed the English Channel, disembarked near Cherbourg, France and prepared to go into action.

I dug a foxhole and I had this prayer session with the chaplain. We could hear the shooting and we knew we were going to go into combat right away. Then someone crawled up and said, "Anybody know anything about medics?" And nobody volunteered. Nobody volunteers for anything in the Army. And then they called my name and gave me a bag and a kit. They put the bag and the kit on my shoulder and put me on a truck and I was in combat.

Just like that, Maury was a medic. He remembers his first day in combat.

Yes, I remember the first time I was in combat. I was walking tall and I learned to walk and bend down a little bit. Every time those shots came by, I learned how to duck real fast – how to stay real low.

He had to learn how to survive in combat and he had to learn how to be a medic.

I had a lot to learn. I was very disturbed about the fact that I had no medical training. Everything that I did was experimental, initially, with all of the soldiers that I came in contact with. And there's something that always troubled me. It's that when a bomb landed, there were fifteen to twenty-five people involved in that area and everybody's bleeding. Some people lost limbs or whatever. Who do you take first? You only have enough in your kit to take care of ten, fifteen, twenty people. You only have so many bandages, so much morphine, so much sulfa. And you have to decide who's going to live or who's going to die. You never know for sure that you made the right decision because blood was all over. Blood was all over. When you see limbs all over the place, I mean, that is – you just can't handle it. I cried. I cried internally. It was a terrible, terrible sight. I never learned to overcome that. My heart was pained with what I saw. And I was scared for my own life. I was no brave guy. I just went.

Medics were unarmed, but they were expected to be in the middle of the fight.

I always was a leader. I always was up front. We learned to walk fifteen to twenty yards behind each other. One day my body just would not go and I trailed everybody till I was at the end of the line. A shell came in and wiped everybody out, except for me and maybe a half dozen other fellas at the end of the line. And you always wondered about that.

Another incident – I'm with a small company and there's a captain and a lieutenant – and the captain said we're going to this area and try to wipe out whoever's there. We want this group to go here and the lieutenant to take the other group the other way. So the lieutenant wanted the medic, but the captain says, "I'm taking the medic." So, I went with the captain and everybody on the other side, with the lieutenant, was wiped out or wounded. They ran into a trap and that was the end of that group.

Maury is Jewish and he encountered some ugly attitudes in the Army.

There was a lot of anti-Semitism at that particular time. There were a lot of people that I came in contact with that had never met Jews. And a lot of people were resentful about the fact that there weren't many Jews on the front line. Remember, we were only one percent of the population. But they felt that more Jews should be on the front line and they resented the fact that there were a lot of Jews that were back home. Initially, I thought I could talk to these people and discuss with them what the situation was and why we were no different than anybody else, but I was never successful in that.

Feren tried to remain faithful to his religion, even on the battlefield.

We had the Day of Atonement. It came in the middle of September. According to Jewish law, you're given dispensation when your life is in danger. But we were in a reserve area and I felt I'm going to try to observe the fast day. I figured that my body would be acceptable to it. So I fasted till about twelve o'clock. And about twelve o'clock, I said to myself, 'You know you're a big fool. If you're called out to fight, you're not going to be able to move around because you won't have any strength.' That's a twenty-four-hour fast and I had already fasted like eighteen hours. And I had dug a foxhole. Even though we were in reserve, we were in a dangerous area. They had a coffee set-up maybe 250 yards away. So I took off my helmet and left all my stuff by my foxhole and I headed over to the area where they had the coffee and some food. And a shell came over right where I was and split my helmet in half and destroyed everything around the foxhole. I was fortunate that I was saved because I had gone away from there.

The stress of being a combat medic took its toll on Maury.

I had battle fatigue twice. In the early part of the war, I remember I was so destroyed emotionally that I went to the captain and I said, "I can't handle it anymore.

Let me off for twenty-four hours or something. Let me just get my senses together. But I want to come back to my outfit," I said. "I don't want to go to the hospital." And I remember laying out in this hospital area, this temporary set-up, whatever it was. I was just laying outside and the sun was shining and I could hear the planes going over. I stayed there for twenty-four hours and then came back to my outfit. The same experience happened someplace near Luxembourg – the same type of experience.

In late 1944, the 5th Division was near the German border.

At Metz, which was in the Alsace-Lorraine area, we ran into a big problem. We had moved too fast for our supplies to reach us. And the German gun emplacements were way up on top of a big hill and they could shoot right down at us. We lost thousands of men in that particular spot there because we were at the bottom of the hill and we couldn't get up there. Every time we sent men up there, they would be shot down and we lost a number of medics. I don't know exactly how many. My medic table of organization was 32 and we turned over to 103 in a year of fighting.

With his outfit losing medics at an alarming rate, Feren felt he had to speak up.

One day we lost maybe two or three medics and I came to the captain and I said, "We absolutely have to change our status because we can't go out there and take care of men. We're just being shot down. They're not respecting our red crosses."

He says, "You're out of line."

I said, "Well, you try it yourself." It was more or less almost a rebellious remark.

So he took a Red Cross flag and we were on the other side of an embankment, which went up like ten or fifteen feet. He crawled over the embankment and came down into this field of fire and they shot a bullet right through his Red Cross flag and he came right back out. So, we started to work at night.

In mid-December of 1944, the German Army launched a massive counter-attack.

The Battle of the Bulge – we came in on the flank. It was December and it was cold. It was almost Christmastime and you just lay in the foxhole. The snow was maybe six inches deep. The weather was about twenty degrees and you couldn't keep yourself dry. We lay in the snow for twenty-one days...lay in the snow for twenty-one days. And the medics took care of people that had frozen feet. I begged the captain to

let the people with the frozen feet go back. He said, "We can't let anybody go back."
And I was so angry at the captain. Their feet were so bad.

The German artillery was relentless.

The bombs kept coming. There's a strange phenomenon with the mind. The bombs come – Bam! Bam! Bam! – and you don't want them to stop because there's a rhythm to it. They stop for five minutes and you're out of rhythm. You're out of sync. It's strange, but you want the bombs to keep coming.

And for Feren, there was a sound that seemed even louder than the explosions.

There was one particular time the bombs were coming in so fast that I could hear my heart going up and down. It never stopped pounding. I could hear it pound. You just didn't know whether you were going to live or die.

Maury remembers the time he was asked to help a soldier who wasn't wounded – physically.

One day the captain came over to me and told me there's a Jewish soldier that is having difficulty adjusting. "He doesn't want to go. He doesn't want to go to the front. I want you to talk to him."

So I went to talk to this young man. I don't know what his name was. I told him that we have to be representative of good Jews, good Jewish-Americans. "It's up to you to show that you're that kind of person."

He says, "I don't want to go. I can't go."

I said, "You've got to go in with a positive attitude. If you're not positive when you go, you're going to die." Unfortunately, he went out the next day and he was gone. He was shot down almost immediately.

In February of 1945, Feren earned a Bronze Star.

Well, we were fighting someplace and there were men that were hit all around me. And somebody was way, way out – maybe a hundred yards away from me. And there were two dead people lying and he was right next to one of the dead. I went to him and there were shots coming from all directions. I crept and crawled and I pulled him over the dead bodies because he couldn't move. I had to pull him on the ground. And remember, at twenty-eight or twenty-nine years old, I was strong. I just pulled him and got him to an area where the litter bearers could take care of him. And you know – you're not feeling too good when you're crawling over dead bodies. I had to crawl over the dead bodies to get there and get back the same way. I never knew that they offered Bronze Stars for anything like that. There's just something that tells you that it's something that you have to do.

Maury was later awarded a second Bronze Star when he rescued another soldier under fire. Feren also received a Purple Heart.

I was wounded in a little village called Etampes. I don't even know where it's at. It was a wooded area and I was hit with shrapnel. They removed most of the shrapnel and I was back on the job in three days.

When he returned, he had a different assignment.

After I was hit, they took me off the line and made me a Jeep driver. I drove the captain and the lieutenant around because they were part of an atrocities search group. They set up an atrocities search group when the war was almost over. It was over in most areas. And we came across seventy-five women who were going to a death camp. That's an experience by itself – liberation. I was a liberator.

For years, Feren was unable to talk about the scenes he witnessed in the Concentration Camps.

It was one of the most horrible experiences of my life. I saw people that were like skeletons – all emaciated. They almost looked animal-like. We offered them food and then we gave them too much food and no doctors were there and in some cases, I think, we damaged their bodies from that. Two or three died. I can never forget that. And we had a mass funeral. There were bodies piled on the side of the highway. They were piled on top of each other. They dug a great big area and they had the whole town come out and they had individual coffins for each person who was buried. I don't know how big that area was. I don't know how many people there were. But I remember that day the sun was shining down on it all. It was a very terrible experience, a very terrible experience.

Maury could barely control his bitterness.

I was terribly angry. I carried that anger with me for many years. I was eaten up inside. I almost created a riot with these Germans when I went to a prison camp. I had so much hate for them. But you get over that.

Maury Feren came home in the summer of 1945 and was discharged from the Army in October. It took a long time for the memories of war to begin to fade.

The horror of war. Initially, for a long while, I could see bodies and people with their limbs off. I once saw somebody with their groin just split in two. The war experience changed your life forever. You develop a different sense of values. You learned about different people. You learned about fear. You learned about being saved. You learned about God, where God comes in the picture. It's a very spiritual kind of thing. And you're also left with the fear that never leaves you. I never go to a Fourth of July fireworks show. I consider it artillery. I can't handle it. I jump. I still jump sixty-some years later when I hear something that sounds like a bomb. That experience never left me.

My father is the inspiration for my involvement in the preservation of these personal stories from World War Two. At a very early age, I learned that my dad, and just about every other father in the neighborhood, served in the war. When I was a child, I wanted him to tell me all he could about that experience and he did share some stories, but he did not go into detail. At the time, he probably figured I was too young to understand much of what he had gone through. I realize now how fortunate I am that he talked at all. I have interviewed dozens of veterans who never told their families about their time at war.

Fortunately, my dad kept a diary during the war. In the States, he made daily entries. After he got overseas, he wrote when he could find the time. Soldiers were ordered not to keep diaries. The concern was that sensitive information might fall into the hands of the enemy, but many wanted a record of their experiences and they ignored the order. My father still had the diary with him (a little red memo book) when he was captured. He hid it during his time as a prisoner of war and dared not write in it. On his way home, he picked up where he had left off and wrote about his time as a POW. More than thirty years later, I encouraged him to finish his story. Thanks to my father's foresight, I have a fairly complete account of his World War Two experience.

Clarence O. Swope
U.S. Army

My dad, known to many as 'Mike,' was drafted into the Army in March of 1943. After basic training, he was assigned to the 75th Infantry Division. For the next several months, he did everything he could to get out of the infantry. He applied for the Army Specialized Training Program and was accepted and attended classes at the University of Wyoming. He enjoyed his time in the A.S.T.P., but it didn't last. On December 27, 1943, he was sent back to the 75th Division. He requested a transfer to the Army Air Force and was accepted for cadet training. He began training in March of 1944. But in May, the invasion of Europe was imminent and all soldiers that had some infantry training were ordered to report back to an infantry outfit. Dad joined the 86th Infantry Division for a short time. Then, he thought he caught a break when he was sent to Camp Howze in Gainesville, Texas to join the 4173rd Quartermaster Depot Company. But a few weeks later, he was transferred to the 103rd Infantry Division (based at Camp Howze) and that was his last stop. He was in the infantry for the duration. Shortly after he joined Company B of the 409th Regiment, he met a soldier named Clayton Rippey. 'Rippey' became his best friend – his foxhole buddy.

In October of 1944, the 103rd 'Cactus' Division shipped out.

Shipping Out

I was aboard the U.S.S. Monticello, an ex-Italian luxury liner – I really mean "ex". I was in "F" hold, about 20 feet below sea level. We had two meals a day (beans and lemonade). "F" hold was extremely hot; the only air we got was from a single tube above. We were allowed on deck two hours in the morning and two hours in the afternoon, but I managed to find a hiding place under a gun turret or someplace on deck, so that when the two hours were up, they couldn't find me to run me off the deck. When the next group came up, I would come out of hiding. It worked every time.

After about 11 days out, we finally saw land. It was the coast of North Africa;

soon we saw Spain and Portugal. We passed through the Straits of Gibraltar; saw the famous "rock", and the spot where the French fleet was scuttled. It was quite a relief when we finally docked at the city of Marseilles in southern France.

Welcome to France

It was night when we got off the ship. There were few lights and they were laying smoke screens over the harbor. There were barrage balloons over the harbor.

We were lining up to get ready for our move to the camping area when a German observation plane flew over. Our anti-aircraft guns opened up on it, but it must have got away. It was quite a sight to see the sky light up with the bursts of flak.

We started moving out on our long march to our camping area, carrying full equipment. All the way through town we would march a little and then rest a little. The French people were all outside the houses, begging for cigarettes, soap, chocolate, chewing gum, or some other hard to get article. We would accommodate them and feel proud to keep up the tradition of the big-hearted Yanks. Of course, if they had a little wine or cognac we wouldn't refuse. They were afraid the American officers would get mad if they got caught giving us wine. Our Lieutenant Crown convinced them that the officers were not so bad. Lou René, my French speaking friend, was our interpreter. He taught me a lot of French on the ship, so I didn't do so bad. The Frenchmen would tell us all their experiences with the Germans, and how they killed and tortured their people.

We finally reached the outskirts of town and it started to rain and my equipment was getting heavier. The boys were dropping out like flies. Finally, I said to Rippey, "Let's drop out and spend the night here." We knew there were still German snipers in the area, but we decided to take a chance.

Rippey woke up first, so when I woke up there was no one around. I walked down the road and saw Rippey sitting by a big fire getting dry. René was with him. A Frenchman with one leg was getting wood for the fire and making coffee. Was that a beautiful sight! So, I warmed up a K-ration and had my breakfast. This Frenchman had lost two daughters and one son to the Germans. They also killed his dog. We were getting ready to start off again for camp, when a Frenchwoman came over and said there were two Germans in a guard tower and they wanted to surrender. So we went casually over and told them to come out unarmed. They did and we had our first two prisoners.

We started for camp and caught a ride on a 'duck.' He took us into camp. The Captain began to chew us out for being lost, so we gave him our prisoners and told him it was a long battle getting these two prisoners.

The camp was a muddy field, but it was our home for a couple of weeks. For a few days we had to go to the docks and help unload ships. It was a good deal because we got plenty of food. We borrowed some candy bars by the dozens; we also got sleeping bags for our squad. Lt. Crown would turn his back when we liberated all this stuff. The officers were allowed to bring a lot more over than the enlisted men, so we didn't feel guilty.

Moving Out

After about a week of doing this and sneaking out to town, we were called together by our Executive Officer, 1st Lt. Thompson (The Head), and he told us that a battalion was pinned down by the Germans up in the Belfort Pass, and we were to get them out. Our company was to go ahead to guide the rest of the outfit to the front. (My first mission.)

We were taken ahead in trucks and placed alone at various intersections to make sure the convoy went through uninterrupted. When the convoy would stop at night, we would be moved ahead to new positions.

We didn't get much sleep. The French treated us pretty good; they gave us anything we wanted. One time, the First Sergeant came along to pick me up and I was sitting on a chair by a fire. A Frenchman had just given me a bottle of Kish (liquid fire) and his daughter was fanning the fire and warming K-rations. I had a sign on a tree with an arrow saying 'This Way.' I guess I was on the job...

Our truck finally came to pick me up; I had my pockets full of wine and whiskey for the guys on the truck. When the truck slowed down I jumped on the tailgate. I had trouble climbing on. I was weighted down with booze. I decided to lay my rifle on the tailgate so I could use both hands getting on. The safety was not on and my rifle went *off and grazed the helmet of Sergeant Moseby, and went through the canvas just above his head. He started hollering at me, so I sent two bottles of booze to him. It didn't take long for him to forget the ringing in his ears.*

We finally got to within 10 miles from the front and we stopped for a couple of days before the push off. We could easily hear the artillery, and we decided we weren't there for an Army of Occupation. There were a lot of mines in the area and we had occasional accidents with them. A few men were killed, but no one from my company.

About the third night there, Clayton Rippey and myself wrote a song called 'After It's Over' and it went over big in the company. The mess sergeant wanted to buy it, but no sale. We willed it to him in case Rippey and myself were killed. Lt. "Bobby" Crown wanted the song, too. We went through the rest of combat singing 'After It's Over' and we had the song 'Paper Doll' down pat, too. We had our own special arrangement of 'Paper Doll.' Rippey and I were very good at harmonizing. Rippey was a swell cartoonist, too. He was a swell morale booster to Company B. We were always making our troubles look like jokes.

The necktie rule, for instance. The Colonel had put out orders when we left Marseilles that we should wear neckties, or at least have them with us. So various times in combat, especially in a tight spot, I would pop up and say, "It's a damned good thing we brought these neckties!"

Combat

Well, it's finally time for our outfit to move up front. Our platoon was left behind two days to guard the regiment's duffel bags. Eventually, we were brought up to our outfit on trucks. They were dug in just behind the lines. It had been raining just about all the time. We had to cross a big river on a footbridge that was under fire by snipers, and we had to walk 10 miles in mud almost knee deep before we caught up with them. They were on the side of a hill. It was so dark we had to hold hands to keep from getting lost. It was pretty stormy that night and the wind blew down a large tree that just missed Rippey and me by inches.

When dawn finally came, we found ourselves with good old B Company again. When it was light enough, we moved up front and relieved some Texas outfit.

The following morning, we were to start our attack. Our Colonel had gotten a medal for relieving an outfit without the Jerries knowing about it, so they didn't know that green troops were about to hit them. Just before our push-off, our artillery opened up with a terrific 10-minute barrage.

The first day we were battalion reserve and we followed close behind in the woods. I saw my first dead American soldier lying in a foxhole in the mountains. I was kind of stirred, but in a few minutes I got over it. Later that day, I saw our first wounded being brought back on jeeps, etc. When we finally stopped for the night, our outfit dug in, in the spearhead position.

During the night, two Jerries came running through our area and Berkowitz, a Jewish boy from Brooklyn, cut them down with an automatic rifle. One of them fell about 10 feet from my foxhole and he hollered and screamed all night long. We had orders not to get out of the foxholes at night, so I couldn't help anyway. I didn't get much sleep that night. He was dead in the morning with 3 bullets in his chest.

We were about ready to push off again, so I picked up a light machine gun with a couple boxes of ammo and decided to carry that for a while. We shoved off early that morning and had gone about 200 yards to the top of a hill when a bunch of Jerries in a house in the valley opened up on us with machine guns. I set up my machine gun and used all my ammo on the house. I guess I quieted a few of them.

Meanwhile, we had sent a squad to take the house and our mortar squad dropped quite a few mortar shells. It took us about 20 or 30 minutes to take over the house. What Jerries were left, finally surrendered. Just after we took the house, a Jerry came riding down a trail on a bike. One of our boys saw him coming so he stepped behind a tree and waited for him. When he got there, our boy yelled halt and the kid was so scared he fell off his bike. He surrendered. He was only about 13 years old, but he had on a German uniform so we took him as a prisoner.

We heard action on the left, so we sent out a patrol to see what was up. It was a bunch of Jerries in a house again. They were firing on G Company up on a hill. Our boys came up behind the house and surprised them. G Company came down from the hill and rushed the building with grenades. Our boys hollered at them, and told them to cease firing. We gave them their prisoners and joined the outfit again.

We moved across a field and hit a road, so we decided to follow it for awhile. I was sent out to the left flank, as a flank guard, in case of any attacks from the side. There were plenty of snipers, and they made it pretty hot for us. One bullet sang off the edge of my steel helmet, and I didn't waste much time getting behind a big tree. I couldn't locate that guy, so we went on. The bad part of fighting in the mountains is that you can't see the snipers.

We went down the road about 100 yards when an 88 shell landed on the road next to me and killed two boys from our outfit. We waited about 10 minutes for more shells to land, but nothing happened so we moved forward again. In a little while, we hit a town. Most of the Jerries had left the town and were dug in on a hill on the opposite side of the town. We took the town with little resistance, and set up on the outskirts below the hill where the Jerries were. We called back for artillery and they opened up with white phosphorus shells and finished with smoke shells to cover our attack on the hill. We took the hill without many casualties from our company.

After driving the Jerries off the hill, we took to the road again and moved out to the right of the town. We had no sooner gotten out of the town when we were caught in the middle of an enemy mortar 88 attack. Barchfield, the B.A.R. man on our squad, got it bad in the shoulder. T/Sgt. Ainsworth went deaf for a while and got hit in the arm. They were about 20 feet from me when they were hit. I found a ditch full of mud at the edge of the road, so that's where I sweated out the barrage. Every time I heard a shell coming I would snuggle down in the muddy water and duck my head under until it hit. I prayed between shells, and I guess all the others did, too. It comes natural.

The barrage seemed to last about half an hour, and left us with about 8 men in our squad. We pulled back to the edge of town to the shelter of buildings and waited for further orders. We had new orders in about a half-hour and I didn't like them no how. We were to cut across country through the hills at night and work ourselves behind the enemy lines. We were to be extremely quiet and not fight unless as a last resort. We were to go 10 miles behind enemy lines and take a town there.

There was a large German column (3,000 men?) moving down a highway towards the town. We were to take that town with about 400 men, set up a roadblock and capture the (3,000?) Germans. I was already so tired I was about to drop, and I was soaked all the way through. All I carried was 3 bandoleers of ammunition, K-rations, my rifle and a few packs of cigarettes. It was so dark I couldn't see my hand in

140

front of my face. But we took off into the woods with B Company leading and our platoon at the head.

Our squad was at the point and I was First Scout. I was supposed to be Second Scout, but Sedeman, our First Scout, was starting to crack so I took over. It's the most nerve-wracking job in the infantry. A First Scout's job is to go ahead of the column and locate enemy resistance. The only way you can do that is by letting them fire on you. So we started out with 400 (?) men. Most of our officers stayed near the rear; we had only two or three with our company. Captain Walton, "Dangerous Dennis", stuck pretty close to me all the way and not very many officers will do that. We started out by compass, so it was really slow moving. Captain Walton would come up every 15 minutes and check compass directions; and then we would move out.

Nobody dared talk and that made it all the worse. All I had to do was think and be scared. After about 3 miles, I was walking along a small ravine and I hadn't heard a sound all night, when all of a sudden a Jerry opened up with a machine gun about 130-150 feet in front of me. We all hit the dirt (mud) and hardly dared to breathe.

Every time the Jerry heard a sound he would open up in that direction. Most of us dived into the ditch calling our names. Captain Walton heard someone on the edge of the ravine about 5 feet from us. The Captain tapped me and whispered, "Who is it?" We breathed again when he said, "Knudson". He was one of our boys.

The Captain wanted me to crawl up towards the machine gun nest and try to knock it out. I suggested that we should go by compass around the machine gun nest and come out behind them. He agreed and the plan worked. We hardly dared to breathe; it was pitch black out there so we had good cover. We backed up about 50 yards and went around the machine gun and came back to our line of travel well behind them.

Now that the machine gun nest was behind us, we were on our way again. We had trouble with snipers from there on. They fired from all four sides of us. Our communications wire ran out, so we had to go ahead with no connections at all with the rear. We kept changing our course to go around the strong points, and finally we got lost. Half the men were lost because of the extreme darkness. They were walking all around the mountains in small groups. We decided the only thing we could do was to stop until it got light enough to move on. We didn't know what would happen in the morning when the Jerries would see us. The Jerry snipers got a lot of our men during the night.

Dawn came and I saw two of my buddies dead, about a few feet from me. We rounded up our men and started out again as soon as we could. We were lucky that day. There were very few Jerries in the area of the mountains we traveled and I was First Scout all day. My K-rations were gone so I didn't eat all day.

About 4 o'clock that afternoon, I spotted four Jerries coming out of the woods with their hands up. So I took them prisoners. A little while later, I came across a small village. I didn't know whether there were any Jerries in there or not, so I called up the Captain. He said to go down into the town and ask the people in the first house if there were any Germans around. So I came down off the hill, across the open field, expecting the Jerries to open up on me any minute. But luck was with me, when I reached the first house; an old French couple was waiting for me with a bottle of wine. Boy, did that hit the spot. I got a couple apples, too.

The rest came down and we walked right through the town with no resistance at all and kept going. The next town was our objective. It was over a large hill. We got on top of the hill and saw our objective. It was a large town, full of Jerries. From the top of the hill we could see Jerries riding cars and motorcycles up and down the main street. A lot of the Germans were walking around with French girls.

We set up our machine guns and mortars on top of the hill and got ready for the attack. My platoon was to come down the bare face of the hill, cross a creek, and start taking the buildings at the right end of town, and work our way towards the center.

At a given signal, our machine guns opened up and the Jerries scattered like rats in a trap. They set up machine guns, etc. in houses and fired back. They got a few of our machine gunners and I believe Lt. Peters from our 3rd platoon got wounded. A machine gunner from D Company caught 3 bullets; one lodged in a metal-faced bible over his heart, another lodged in a thick wallet over his right side, and the third bullet caught him in the finger. One of those lucky guys whose time wasn't up yet.

About five minutes after we opened up, our platoon started down the hill and a hail of Jerry tracers followed us down. One tracer bullet hit the barrel of my rifle and bounced off my trigger finger, taking the skin off 2 knuckles. When we reached the bottom of the hill, we had to cross a swift flowing creek. It was a tough obstacle, but *we made it. Although we were dripping wet with water, (and me with 2 jackets, 2 shirts, 2 sweaters, and 2 pair of pants so soaked full of water I could barely walk) we made it.*

We finally reached the first building, tossed a few grenades through a window, and went in. It was empty. About that time, Rippey, who didn't know we were in the building, let go with a bazooka, but luckily it didn't go off.

We started to work our way towards the center of town, searching all of the buildings and taking a lot of prisoners. They would fire on us until we got right up to them and then they surrendered.

After about an hour the town was ours, so we planned our defensive and planned to spend the night there. We had no communications with the rear, no food besides what little the French had, and we only had a few medical aid men to care for all our wounded and very little medical supplies. We were surrounded by Germans on 4 sides. We had a couple of walkie talkies, but we were out of range. Walkie talkies weren't much good anyway. They called all night trying to make connections with the rear. We needed blood plasma for our wounded, and there was no way to get it.

We had captured a German doctor and he helped out a lot. He had some surgical equipment with him, and he did a lot of operating that night. The first part of the night was quiet with very little action. Every time one of us would step outside a building, a sniper would take a shot at us, but they were too far to see good, so they were not very accurate.

I spent the first part of the night drying my clothes. About 2 o'clock in the morning, I was sent out to guard a roadblock on the far end of town. There were about seven of us on the roadblock. We had a German truck parked cross ways across the road. A squad of the second platoon was dug in along the edge of the road leading to the roadblock. I guess they were plenty nervous. Earlier in the night, a Jerry walked down the road right by them. Sgt. Moseby, the last man, halted him and shot him. The Jerry had walked past the whole squad, so they weren't taking any chances now. They shot my Assistant Squad Leader in the shoulder, and they were taking shots at almost everyone they saw. So we sent a man ahead to warn them that a relief guard was coming.

We finally reached the roadblock and we set up our guard. Two men sat in the truck, two men were under it with a machine gun, and a B.A.R. man, another rifleman, and myself were along the side of the road behind a wall that came up flush with the road. A hill came down flush with the opposite side of the road.

We were there a short time when all hell broke loose. A bunch of Jerries were coming down the hill just across the road, and opened up on us at about 30 yards. We opened up on them. They threw a grenade on the hood of the truck and got the two guys in the truck cab. I think one was Sedeman. Then they started rolling grenades across the road, down on us. I threw 3 grenades up at them, and must have got a few. They rolled 3 grenades down that landed about 10 feet from me. One of them landed right next to me and wounded the guy on the other side of me. I never even got scratched.

The two guys from under the truck came down by me, they were wounded. There were two of us left and I was almost out of ammunition. Finally, some of the boys in the battalion aid station, which was set off the road about 75 yards behind me, opened up and helped us. The Jerries shot a bazooka shell at the building and got about six guys with it, none too serious. Finally, I told Portio (the guy left with me) that we should try to make it back to the battalion aid station, where we could hold them off better. We would have been dead ducks for their grenades if we had stayed behind the wall, but we had to cross an open field to get to the aid station. One more grenade on us made us decide to take the chance. I covered Portio when he made a break, and he got in the door with a hail of bullets following him. I figured it would be best if I went in another way because they had the door covered, so I made a dash for a small window that was even with the ground. I dove headfirst at the window, after criss-crossing the field to keep out of fire. I hit the window with my helmet, did a somersault and landed in a watering trough for horses in the basement. So, after all the trouble I took drying my clothes earlier in the evening, it turned out to be a waste of time. I was wet again. I groped around the basement shouting my name so they wouldn't fire on me. Finally, I came to the basement room where many of our wounded were, and I worked my way through them and went upstairs.

We fired back for about 10 more minutes, and finally they quit firing back, so we stopped and a few guys and myself crawled out and brought our wounded in. There were 6 or 7 of us still able to fight so we put guards on all sides of the building. I got *stuck with the front of the building facing the Jerries. I was seeing shadows for the rest of the night, but I guess they had left. At least it was quiet for the rest of the night.*

The wounded men moaning kind of got on my nerves. Lt. Peters had a very bad leg and it was driving him nuts. One of my best buddies, Frank Sedeman, had a bad hole in his arm, and he never mentioned it until the seriously wounded were taken care of. Then he nonchalantly asked the medic to patch him up. My Assistant Squad Leader, Corporal Lehrman, was shot in the arm by one of our own men during the excitement. He came walking into the aid station and said, "Someone stuck one in my arm. Any chance of getting it patched up?" It is really indescribable the way our boys took it that night.

Well, finally, after years of minutes, dawn started to break and it was a relief to see what was going on. It was a relief to our medics to work by sunlight, instead of flashlight. I guess everybody felt a little better. Some of the boys that were in town were out walking around now, and we reorganized and got ready to meet the retreating Germans that we had cut off.

About 6 o'clock in the morning, an Indian boy from the weapons platoon was doing something with the machine gun under the truck on the road. A Sergeant of the weapons platoon, I believe it was Sgt. Cass, was standing in front of him. The machine gun went off accidentally and caught Sergeant Cass in the legs. We rushed to him and started to give him first aid, but he went into shock before we could get him the 75 yards to the aid station and he died a few minutes later.

The same morning one of our boys, who was lost in the woods the night before, came in and he cracked. He kept screaming and hollering all the time.

We sent out a small patrol to find the Jerries that were retreating toward us. About an hour later, a very large Jerry column headed by high-ranking officers came toward us with their hands in the air. They had given up to our small patrol without a fight. They must have figured a couple of divisions were around the town. Later that day, an American patrol came to our town from a small town not far away and said our troops had broken through and were hunting for us.

We immediately sent a patrol for medical supplies, and they came back with the much needed blood plasma. We tried to radio back and have doctors flown in by Cubs, but we couldn't get anywhere. Later that night, our vehicles broke through with food and ammunition and it wasn't long before the whole outfit caught up to us and we had a rear line again.

The next day we shoved off again with my outfit in the lead, and I was First Scout again. We went over a small mountain, and followed a railroad track leading to the next town. We were bothered by snipers and occasional machine gun nests, but we didn't hit any large forces. Some of the sniper bullets came pretty close. I realize now why I was born such a short guy. We finally came to the main road leading to the town we were to take. We spread out on both sides of the road and started in. As soon as we got close to the town, we took to the hills and after an artillery barrage we took the town with little resistance.

As usual I got stuck on a roadblock again; the rest of the outfit searched the houses, all but the one next to me. It wasn't long before a German car came down the road. We opened up on it and got an officer who was driving it. He tried to run, but we cut him down. There were five of us on the roadblock. The car he was driving was full of silk stockings from a nearby factory, and a sack of regimental mail.

Soon after that a German messenger came down the road on a motorcycle and he got upset with a bullet in the head. I claimed the motorcycle and I played around with it for awhile trying to get it to go. Finally, I got disgusted and sold it to Jack Coleman, a boy in my squad, for a candy bar. He got it running early the next morning. So I borrowed it to run back and forth to the C.P. I had a wild time at first. It would go like hell, but I couldn't stop it. Half the time I was in the part of town that wasn't searched yet and the snipers tried to get me, but the way I was zigzagging from sidewalk to street, it was impossible. After a little practice, I got used to it.

About 7 or 8 o'clock the following morning, the French lady that lived in the house across from our roadblock came out and said there were Jerries in the basement who wanted to surrender. So we took them and found out they had enough guns and equipment to last all day. They could have easily killed us all at the roadblock.

We took it easy and moved out after a couple hours. We had fairly level ground for a change, and it sure was a relief. We moved across fields and hit quite a bit of scattered resistance. We were heading for another town. One of our other regiments failed to take it the day before. As soon as darkness came we took to the main road with orders to fire on no one unless absolutely necessary. The whole battalion was behind us, and we were scattered all along the road.

A Jerry car was coming up on us from the rear. Everybody froze where they were, and the car passed through the whole battalion. When it reached the front, where I was, someone opened up on it. It swerved and came to a stop right next to me. A Jerry Colonel and another officer were in it. The Colonel started to get out and he started to draw a pistol on me. I didn't see him, but Sgt. Milosek did, and he shot him just in time.

Captured

We went on and finally came to the town. The town (Selestat) was on the opposite side of a river and there were a few houses on this side of the river. The buildings were full of Jerries, and it took quite a time to get them out. We used up all our bazooka ammunition on machine gun nests in the houses. We finally cleared our side of the river and were to cross the bridge, and take the town on the other side. Our company was to cross the river first, and the rest of the battalion would cross later. We made it O.K. and took the first 3 or 4 buildings in town. We then set up a defensive and sent out searching patrols. They were bringing in prisoners all night long. The date was December 1, 1944.

The building I was in was the first one across the river on the right side. We were overlooking the main road and the bridge. We picked off a few Jerries we saw coming down the road. They opened up with 88's and mortars and most of the shells were landing much too close to be comfortable.

About 2 a.m. on December 2nd, we heard tanks coming down the road and the fellows said it was probably our own T.D. outfits. As they got closer, we could hear that they were coming from the opposite direction of our troops, so we kept watching. Pretty soon we could make out 4 or 5 tanks coming toward us; they were enemy tanks. We took to the buildings, most of them empty. We fired on the tanks and tried to scare them off. It turned out to be what seemed like a whole division, so we were caught red-handed without any anti-tank weapons. We could pick off the accompanying infantry, but we couldn't scratch the tanks. We kept fighting, but they came right up on us.

I was in the building nearest the river near the bridge. I went to the other end of the building and told the guys not to shoot; we had no defense against the tanks, let them go through us. They lined up three tanks in front of the buildings and one tank was sitting on the bridge. I was in a room only about 30 yards from the river. I was tempted to swim across the river, but when I looked out the window the tank crew saw me and started to lower the gun and aim at the window. I ran to the back wall and climbed behind a heat stove. Then all hell broke loose. The stones were collapsing all around and I was buried in a pile of rubble. I must have been knocked out. When I came to I was buried in a pile of cement and bricks. The Jerries were in the room throwing grenades around. I caught a few pieces, but I was so numb I couldn't feel it. My shoulder and back ached pretty bad. I must have passed out for a while; when they saw me they dug me out of the rubble and took me outside. I was pretty dazed and didn't know what had happened.

I saw some of our boys standing outside the building across the street with their hands over their heads. Their buildings had been surrounded and knocked down, too. They brought out one of our officers on a door. It looked like his legs were practically shot off. He was covered with a blanket. I happened to remember seeing an arm sticking out of the ruins of our building. It was too late to go back, but I later heard it may have been my Assistant Scout Corbiel. I also heard that T/Sgt. Burnett was killed.

I thought my best buddy, Rippey, was killed, too, but I later found out that he made a miraculous escape. When the Jerries entered the building he was in, they threw grenades and he kept running from room to room. Finally, he opened a door and stepped forward only to find himself in a heap in the basement of the building. He groped around and found a pile of turnips. He buried himself with the turnips and stayed there for three days. I later heard that he got out and made it back to American lines.

My platoon Sergeant, S/Sgt. Perkins, made it back and he was later commissioned 2nd Lt. My ex-platoon Sgt. Moseby made it back, too. Later I found out that a regiment was practically wiped out trying to take the town that my company tried to take. My company got further than the regiment did. It took two divisions, the 45th and another, to hold the ground my company had taken. So we didn't do so bad after all.

POW

I was only on the front lines about a month, but when I was there, things came so fast and furious that I have forgotten some of the engagements. I've written a few of them down, but I can only remember parts of others so I didn't mention them. Some were worse, some not so bad, but none of them was a picnic.

After they had rounded up what was left of the company, the Germans started to line us up. A German soldier came over to the line of survivors and was looking for the guy that stole his watch when he was captured. He had a couple of German soldiers with him. He said if he didn't get his watch he would kill all of us.

Just about then, a German tank stopped next to us and the tank commander asked what was going on. The soldier told him someone stole his watch and he would execute us if he didn't get it back. The tank commander said, "Do you mean to tell me that this group of soldiers tried to do battle with my tank division? They deserve a better fate; send them to the rear without harm."

After they rounded up the 20 or so men that were left, they started to march us out of town. We had only gone about 100 yards when we were caught in the middle of one of our own artillery barrages. We all dove for the nearest holes. The Jerries had emplacements dug all along the road; I headed for one of them. I dove into a hole and a Jerry guard landed on top of me. The shells were landing all around us. It must have lasted 15 minutes. Shrapnel got the Jerry on top of me, so thanks to him I came through another close one.

When the barrage ended, we started marching again. Dawn was starting to break and our P-40's came out that morning. All day long they would bomb and strafe the towns ahead of us. We passed through several towns that day. We would wait outside the town and watch our planes dive bomb it. When the bombing was through, we would start through the town. Flak got a few of our planes. It was really a spectacular sight. We spent the night in a small barn, and I finished up the last of my K-rations. The next day we started marching again and soon came to a small town where the Jerry command was located.

We were taken to a school building with a fence around the yard. We were taken out, one at a time, searched and questioned. None of us told them anything, but they knew what outfit we were from, and where we had been. After that we started marching again; by now we were pretty hungry. We came to a large town on the Rhine River where the bridge had been blown out, so we crossed on barges attached to cables. They took us to a large barn and said we would stay there until we could get transportation to a prison camp. We stayed there about three days. Every morning they would give us a small chunk of bread for the day. During the day, they would take us back across the river and make us dig gun emplacements for them. Before they took us to where we were to dig, they would go out of their way to take us through a couple towns so the people could see the American prisoners. We called them propaganda walks. We didn't mind the people laughing and sneering at us, but we were hungry and our legs were about to give out.

All the Jerries that could speak English would ask us if we remembered when Roosevelt had said that, "No American boy would set foot on foreign soil." And they asked us why we were fighting England's war. They said we had no business there.

After about one week there, we were marched to a railroad station and put on boxcars. There were close to 50 men on my car and there was only room for about 30. We had to take turns standing up. We had one pail in our car that was used for a toilet. We were in the car 7 days and the pail was filled up the first day. We had been given a slice of bread about 4 inches square for the first 2 days. They said we would get more food along the way, but we didn't so we made the bread last 2 days and went the other 5 days without. We were given a small chunk of raw hamburger meat during those other five days, but it only caused dysentery.

About the third day on the boxcar, our interpreter, Newmeister, was shot through the head by a German guard and dumped along the side of the railroad tracks. The train moved about 15 miles a day. It stopped for air raids and a little bit of everything. We got water 2 times during the 7 days. I was beginning to get a taste of prison life.

Stalag XII-A

We finally reached Stalag XII-A, Limburg, Germany. We were herded to a large tent with a muddy floor, and stood around hungry and weak. Finally, they took us and gave us a cold shower and took most of our clothes and gave us prisoner clothes. They took my rubber boots and gave me a pair of wooden shoes. Then they gave us a blanket about 3 & 1/2 feet square. Finally, they gave us a bowl of cold grass soup and gave us a place to sleep on the floor of the building. The building was so crowded, I could barely roll over.

I stayed at Stalag XII-A at Limburg about a week; later we found we were fed better there than at any other camp. For breakfast we had a cup of tea and a 3 inch slice of bread, and for supper we had a bowl of grass soup with potatoes in it, and each night we would get a part of a Red Cross parcel. Once a week a small candy bar was given out and we were allowed 3 cigarettes a day. Some of the boys traded off their clothes and jewelry for cigarettes or bread. I gave one of my sweaters for a pack of cigarettes. There was a P.X. in this camp and cigarettes were used as money. Everything was priced at so many cigarettes. Money was useless there.

When we were interrogated, the confidence man in Limburg told us to say we were cooks, butchers or bakers to make sure we didn't qualify for war work. We were told to try to get into a work camp because, according to the Geneva Convention, workers got extra rations. The confidence man that told us that was later executed for collaborating with the enemy. He was right about the rule but wrong on a lot of other things. However, the rule didn't hold true in my case. Limburg was the best camp as far as food and work.

After about a week in Limburg, a group of us were told we were to be transported to a labor camp where the food was better. We were taken to a railroad siding and loaded on boxcars. No heat, no windows, a few cracks in the boards to see out, and one small can for a toilet. When we were waiting on the siding, some stray bombs from an air raid hit the prison camp; we were told they hit the officer barracks.

We must have been on the siding about a day; we could see troop trains on the main line. Most of those cars were painted as International Red Cross cars, but we could see all the Germans on the trains. After about 5 days in the boxcars, most of the time on sidings, and living on one slice of bread a day, the hunger pangs changed to just a lump in my chest.

The weather was below freezing most of the time; everyone had numb legs, so we knew we couldn't last much longer. The train stopped in what seemed an open field, *but in the field was a lone building, which we were told was a hospital. As soon as we entered the hospital we were told to form lines. The line on one side was to get cold showers and the other line hot showers. We all had severe frostbite. I believe I was in the line getting hot showers, and it turned out to be the right line, as it saved my legs. A majority of the guys in the other line had their legs amputated.*

We were then sent into other rooms where there were German doctors; one of them was injecting gasoline into the blood stream of some of the guys. Other doctors were doing experiments. I went into another room, but I do not remember what they did to me. There was a blank period from that time to Christmas Eve that I could never account for.

Stalag IV- C

I pick up in Stalag 4-C on Christmas Eve. I recall receiving a Red Cross parcel during the day on Christmas Eve. We decided to have some kind of Christmas Eve service; we passed the word around and got permission to use an empty tent. About a dozen of us gathered together in the tent, and we asked for a volunteer to lead us. Finally, a very young soldier stood up and said he would. The prayer was for the safety and comfort for our families and loved ones back home. Not one prayer was said to save us or protect us. It seemed as though we all knew we had nothing to fear; and we had an extreme feeling of security and well being. It was all ad-libbed, but it seemed he was saying our thoughts. It was the most moving religious experience I ever had. I only wish I could find words to describe it. The worst was yet to come as far as my POW life, but I don't recall ever being afraid.

Kamnitz Labor Camp

After a few more days at 4-C, about 200 of us were sent via boxcar and truck to a small town in the Sudetenland near the Elbe River. The main street looked like a Christmas card and especially with all the blue streetlights for blackout purposes.

Our building was a two-story building sitting all alone in a field a couple hundred yards from the town. We were on the main road leading to Dresden, which was 30-40 miles east of us. The building had a tall fence around it. We were given one slice of bread in the morning, and 8 men shared a loaf of bread. We could take turns slicing the bread (black bread). The cutter had the last choice of pieces, so it would take quite some time to cut up the loaf. The loaf was about 12 inches long.

In the evening, we were given a bowl of rutabaga soup, mostly water. We also had a cup of tea in the morning. This was heavy workers' rations.

Our Lager Fuehrer was called 'Scar Face.' We asked the other guards what their names were and then we told them how the English would pronounce them. One was F-Face, one was Pri-Head, and there was good old Sh-Head. They would smile when we called them by their English names.

The guards were of the home guard. The home guards were too old for the army, so they were given jobs as prison guards. Near the end, our men were starving and dying. One day I was walking along beside a guard going to work.
He said, "I would love to have you over to my house for dinner. We have very little food for ourselves." But the camp commander had to be the meanest man in Germany. If I saw him today, I would kill him.

Getting back to the first full day there; we were marched about 6 miles to an industrial type area which was all built into a mountainside except for a few smaller buildings and a final assembly area for bombers which was under camouflage netting. We had to climb the mountainside to get there. It took all the strength we had to get there. It was January; we climbed the mountain with wooden shoes with cloth straps. As it turned out, those wooden shoes insulated better in the snow than leather or rubber would have.

By the time we got there the first day, we were completely exhausted. We couldn't see how we could possibly work all day and still expect to walk home to camp at night. Most of us made it, but I don't know how.

About the third or fourth day, I recall returning to camp and there was one steep hill on the road just before camp. I was completely exhausted and had absolutely no strength to climb that hill. I raised my head and said, "God, I can't make that hill. If you're going up, please take me with you." I immediately felt a sensation in my muscles and my legs started moving like I was a robot powered by a motor. Needless to say, we held hands the next few months.

Our job was to dynamite tunnels inside the mountain; spurs were made off the main tunnels which would open up into large rooms where the German engineers and scientists would work. We would load the rocks after the blast into small mining trucks on tracks that led outside, to be dumped over a cliff. We had to be very careful not to be cut on anything; our blood was getting thin and would not clot.

One time, I was pushing a cart and I saw when I came to the opening that a German bomber was being brought out of a building and under the netting for some final fitting. The tail section was hanging over the tracks. One of the guys with me gave the cart a big push and we quickly took off inside the tunnel. We went into one of the spur tunnels that was under construction. I don't know whether they knew where we were, but a short time later the mouth of the tunnel was blasted closed. The rocks filled the openings. We crawled up the pile on the inside and managed to squeeze through a small opening at the top. After getting out, we mingled with the rest until quitting time, then made the long walk back to camp.

The weather was getting a little warmer. The winter had been the worst in Germany that year. We had several tries to escape from the camp, but none were successful. We were too far from our lines, and we were too weak to travel. The camp Commander told us all were killed after recapture.

I had two friends in camp that I trusted; Frank Kirk of Chicago and Tony Stinziano from Wickliffe, Ohio near my home. Tony got up for roll call one morning and stood across from me in the line. I looked at his eyes and they were glazed; he was dead on his feet. I screamed and swore at him to try to bring him back. I told him he promised me a spaghetti dinner when we got home. His expression was absolutely blank. When roll call was made, he did not step forward. He was actually dead on his feet.

Tony was taken to a nearby hospital, never to be seen again. In fact, there was no hospital. I was given his belongings to take home to his family. Tony only had his wallet with pictures of his family. He willed to me some food he had hidden.

Frank Kirk from Chicago was always wheeling and dealing, trading for food. He would share any food he got with me. I gave him my watch that my mother gave me before going overseas. He traded it for food enough for a whole meal, the best meal I ever had.

Every morning going to work Frank and I would sing 'Thanks for the

Memories.' The other guys were so taken by the song that we had to sing the same song on the way to work every day.

Near the end of the war, Frank's eyes were glazed and I'm afraid the same thing happened to him as what happened to Tony.

On Sunday, which was our day off, I decided to read the Bible. I was getting weak and needed help. I just happened to open it to the 23rd Psalm. It seemed to fit my problems; I had been walking in the shadow of death. My nostrils were enlarged and I had an extreme sense of smell. I could smell fresh water for quite a distance. My sense of smell was so strong I could smell things in the fields that I knew were edible.

The war was coming to an end. Dresden had been bombed by American planes. It was a daylight raid. I was working outside on the railroad bed in the valley when we heard an air raid signal. We were put into a shed. I looked out the window and saw bombers flying very high almost from horizon to horizon. They filled the sky; I never saw so many planes in one group. Dresden was about 30 miles east of us; we heard the rumble of bombs for a long time. The guards told us the English and Americans had demolished Dresden. Dresden was a cultural city and not involved with heavy manufacturing. I later found it was the worst bombing in history.

About two days later, the people that evacuated Dresden were coming by on the main road, just outside the POW camp. They had wagons loaded with family and furniture. Their faces were emotionless. They drove their horses practically non-stop. Many horses dropped dead in the front of our camp. The people in town were fighting to get the meat of the horses. We asked the guards if they could get some for our soup. We did get a horse's head and I asked the cook for a piece of meat. He gave me a horse's eye. I decided to bake it inside our coal stove. I set it on a ledge in the oven. It smelled good while it was cooking but when I tried to eat it I could only make a dent in it, so I sold it to another guy for a cigarette.

Escape

One morning the camp commander lined us up for roll call and made us an offer. If we would join the German Army, we would get warm clothes and all we could eat. He said those who wanted to join should step forward. Not one man stepped forward. He ranted and raved and told us the war was coming to an end and German headquarters had sent orders to execute all POW's. We were taken outside the barracks and lined up in front of a firing squad. While he was talking, we heard a noise of low flying airplanes. It didn't take long for them to open up on us and the town next to us. Some POW's ran back inside the barracks. One of the guards opened up the gate to run to his house in town. I followed him out and ran to the town near the camp. The others ran to the barracks for cover. I got to town and went behind the buildings for cover.

I saw some planes coming in from the south. The way the Americans would strafe a town was to come out of the sun, drop their bombs and open up with machine guns. These were Russian planes and they were coming in real low from both sides, right at each other. When they got close they would tilt their wings sideways to avoid a collision. They were nuts. Bullets were hitting all around me. They finally moved on to other targets and I made my way to the other side of town, found an empty building and spent the night there.

I came out the next morning and looked around to figure my next move. I started walking away from town and saw a German woman setting up a table in her backyard. She waved me over. Two political prisoners saw her and headed that way. She set the table and went back to the house. It didn't take long for me to finish my meal but the two political prisoners just pecked at their food and only ate a little bit of each thing. I looked in their eyes and they looked wild. They were completely out of it. I'm sure their minds were going real fast.

Just after the meal I heard some tanks coming down the road. They were Russian tanks. So, now I have another decision to make. Our camp commander had told us that Germany had lost the war, but there would now be a war between Russia and America because there could be no two great powers. The Russians would now be our enemies.

I thought – the Russian soldiers I came across would stick up for us. One time I was working on a railroad bed. Our guards were on our backs because we worked very slow. A group of Russian prisoners from an Air Force camp had hollered at the guards to take it easy on us. They told them that in America all is done with machinery, they don't do hard work. Another time we were walking to work when a truck came by full of potatoes and Russians on the back. They threw potatoes off the truck to us even though our guards were shooting at them. (I had offered a cigarette to one of them. He opened the packet of cigarette papers, threw the papers on the ground, and rolled his cigarettes with the cover for the papers.)

After thinking it over, I decided to try to hitch a ride on one of those Russian tanks. So, I went down to the road and started thumbing a ride. One tank finally stopped and called me over. One Russian popped out of the tank and lifted me on the back of the tank. He gave me a cigarette. Then another Russian popped out of the tank turret and gave me some candy. I knew now that the Russians were my friends.

I told them I was going to the American lines. I rode the tank until we came across a road; they had to make a turn on the road so they left me off about a mile from the intersection and told me which way to go to the American lines. It was getting late in the day; I was still hungry, tired and weak. We had just passed a bombed out German convoy of trucks, with no one around, so I walked back to the trucks, and was looking for food and a place to sleep. I had an extreme sense of smell at the time. I smelled honey on one of the trucks, so I managed to climb on the truck. There were barrels full of honey. I opened one and ate until I got my fill. It was early spring and warm, so I laid on the grass until morning. I had diarrhea in the morning, but the honey made me feel stronger. It was probably the best move I made.

I walked up to the intersection hoping I could get a ride in the direction I was headed. A French couple came along and I asked for a ride. They were driving a horse-driven wagon. They came from Dresden and were trying to get back to France, which was their home. They were an acrobatic troupe in Dresden when the bombs hit. At first they hesitated for fear they would be caught with a prisoner. I told them I would hide under the hay in the wagon. They finally agreed and I was on my way again.

We finally got to the Elbe River and a bridge leading to Prague, the capital of Czechoslovakia. We were stopped and they found me under the hay. I told them I was an American looking for the American lines. They allowed me to cross, but not the French couple.

Prague

I met with another escapee, an American prisoner from another camp. There were empty trucks all around, so we decided to borrow one and cross the bridge to Prague. It happened to be a maintenance truck. As we crossed the river on the bridge, we looked down and saw Germans being strapped to barges. Oil was poured over them and they were burnt alive.

When we got to the other side of the river, we were in Prague. The people in Prague were revolting that day against the Germans who had occupied the city during the war. The people were celebrating like New Year's Eve. They lined the walks on both sides of the very wide street. We kind of got caught up in the spirit. We decided to see what was in the truck that we could throw out as souvenirs. I found a bin of locks, so I sat on the tailgate throwing out locks to the people along the way. I don't recall if there were keys with them or not, but the people were the happiest bunch of people I have ever seen. When I ran out of locks, I looked in the back of the truck to see what was there and found 3 or 4 bags full of American money which was probably confiscated from Americans. I would bring up one bag at a time and throw the money to the people lining the walks until all the money was gone. (I did have afterthoughts later, but I had no regrets. The people were wonderful.)

I started asking people where the American lines were. They said go to the big building at the end of the street, they would know. It was the capitol building. The other guy stayed in the truck and I walked up the steps to the rotunda. I was asked what I was there for. I told them I was an American and trying to find the American lines. He took me down the long hall to the President's office. I was met by the President and told him I was looking for the American lines. He told me they were in Pilsen, but I should not try to get there because there was a tank battle going on along the main road. He said I could stay in his office until morning when we could get more information. He told me I should be hospitalized, I was mostly skin and bones. He got me some food, and he told me again he would take me to the hospital. He said he would like to show me what the Germans did to the women in a nearby town. I believe the town was Ladice (?) about 30 miles from the capital. He said the Germans bulldozed all the buildings to the ground. They executed most of the men, and many of the women had their breasts removed and other tortures. The children that looked like Germans were taken and given to German families to be raised as Germans. The injured women were brought to the hospital in Prague and the President wanted me to go to the hospital with him, so he could show me what they had done to the women.

I believe the reason he wanted me to see what happened to the women was because he was sure I saw the Czech people burning the Germans on the barges and he was embarrassed for what his people were doing. He kept apologizing for the way his people acted. He said he couldn't control them.

Morning finally came; I had slept a few hours in his office. The President checked with his staff to see if the tank battle was over. He said very little battle was going on between Prague and Pilsen. So, I told him I would get in the truck and head for Pilsen. I left his office and went through the rotunda and there were women setting up tables and they were full of Christmas pastries. They had heard the rumor that an American was talking to the President in his office, and it got blown out of proportion. They thought the Americans were going to occupy Prague, which they preferred to Russian rule. I had hoped the Americans would occupy Prague, but it turned out to be the Russians who did. The Czechs were such happy people when they got rid of the Germans, and now they are under Russian rule.

I found the truck outside the capitol building, and the other American sleeping in it. I told him we were only 30 or 40 miles from Pilsen where we would find the Americans.

Back to the American Lines

The tank battle was slowing down; there was still a little action but nothing too close to us. We got about one mile from the American troops, when a jeep came out to see who we were. We said we were coming from a German prison camp. He looked at us, and said, "Who did this to you?" I told him a camp near Kamnitz. The Lieutenant and the Sergeant took off beyond the demilitarized lines. I hope they didn't get themselves messed up. We were taken about 3 miles behind the front lines, and came to a company of men camping there. The first thing they did was take us to their mess hall. We were given milk and white bread. I thought the milk was eggnog and the white bread was angel food cake.

POW's were coming in every once in a while. There was another river parallel to the road. There were POW's walking along the road, and for some unknown reason I saw 6 of them walk right into the river and drown themselves.

I was starting to get confused myself. My mind was so clear prior to reaching the American lines, now I was not sure who I was – a POW or a soldier. We were taken to a building where they gave us food and canned food to take with us. We were taken by truck to the airport, and redistribution center at Regensburg, Germany.

We had our choice of getting fed or going to the delousing chamber. The lice had been driving me crazy. They were everywhere there was hair on my body. One of the best feelings I've ever had was getting rid of the lice. I went to the chow line and got a meal. Then I decided to lay down and sleep for awhile on the ground. There was very little meat on my bones and they would get very sore if they bumped other bones in my legs. I tried lying on my back, but there were bones there, too.

Ike

I was sent over to the Supply Sergeant to get American clothes. I had to get in a line and wait. While I was standing in line, I saw a plane coming in. It had General Eisenhower's stars on it – I was waiting in line to get an Eisenhower jacket. General Eisenhower got into a jeep and he had a truck following him. It had a movie-camera on the top of the cab. They were driving along a road that was raised above the path I was on leading to the supply house. The jeep and truck stopped right above me. General Eisenhower got out and came down the slope where I was standing. After talking to a couple other guys, he came over to me and asked what outfit I was with. I told him General Patch. He said, "Oh yes, you men had some tough battles." He asked me did I get fed? I said, "Yes, but how come we always get boiled, unseasoned chicken?" He said the people running the mess hall were told to feed you that because it was the easiest thing to digest in your condition.

General Eisenhower told me I should be hospitalized until I got stronger. I told him I wanted to go home. He said if I let his aide take me to a doctor, and he says I can travel, he would see to it that I'd get the next ship home. I agreed, but I told him I wanted to get my jacket first. He smiled and said, "O.K."

I also told him he should shut down the Red Cross donut stand. The guys were eating donuts until their stomachs burst. He sent a Lieutenant right away to close it, but it had already closed down.

General Eisenhower raised his hand to salute me, and I stood there in a slump. Finally, I realized I was standing in front of the highest-ranking officer in the Army. So I tried to straighten up to salute him. He gave me the big salute and gave that famous Eisenhower smile. His complexion was so smooth; I had pictured him older, until he took off his hat. He was mostly bald.

Making me stand at attention woke me up to the fact that I was still a soldier. It took out a lot of the fog in my mind. I went back to my tent after getting my new clothes, and saw a guy in the tent next to mine. He had hung himself on the ridge pole. So I got in the chow line, ate my lunch, then went over and told them at camp headquarters that a guy had hung himself.

Coming Home

I decided to take a walk to the Airport Terminal when I heard someone call my name. It was Sergeant Moseby; he came over and held me in his arms and cried like a baby. He had thought he lost his whole company. I remembered one night during combat; we were pinned down on a hill overlooking a town with a guard tower on one end. We were completely out of food. Without anyone knowing it, Sgt. Moseby snuck down to the town and managed somehow to bring back enough food for all of us. From that time on, there was nothing we wouldn't do for him.

Well, I finally got to the air terminal and I heard music for the first time in 6 months or more coming from the terminal speakers. It was "Chiribiribin" by Harry James. Tears came to my eyes; it was the first time I could cry in 6 months. They started playing more music and I got very confused again. The orchestra and violins sounded O.K., but the songs I had never heard before. Finally, I realized the songs I remembered were now out of style and a whole new range of songs were now popular. While in the POW camp, we had no music or radio, no contact at all with the outside world, no letters either.

I got a C-47 to Camp Lucky Strike; it had previously been used for paratroopers. We got on the plane, had boxes to sit on, and bullet holes to see out. We flew in a flight with three C-47's. We finally got up and it seemed O.K. until we got to some mountains. The planes were hitting an updraft and we would look out the bullet holes and watch our wings flap, and see other planes bouncing around. I should have gone with Eisenhower. We finally landed at Camp Lucky Strike, at the port of Le Havre, France. We had a meal and were given a tent to use until our names were called for shipping home. We were given back pay, and a lot of guys were playing cards or dice. I have never seen so much money on one table. I got to talking to one of the card players and he wanted me to go to a supply tent and buy some candy bars. They were $10.00 each. (Some Supply Sergeant was making a killing.) Every time he bought candy bars, he would buy two for me.

My name was called for shipping home – the first ship out! I got my duffel bag and headed for the gangplank. I looked at the steep gangplank and tried to go up. I was still too weak to climb with the bag. I stood there for a while trying to figure out how to get up the gangplank when a Captain came by and asked what was wrong. I told him, "I can't go home. I can't climb the gangplank."

The Captain took my duffel bag and threw it over his shoulder, grabbed my arm and said, "Come on, soldier, you're going home."

We docked at New York and I went to Camp Kilmer and got my leave papers and train fare home.

I arrived in Cleveland and took a taxi to my home. When I got home, my mother was standing on the porch screaming, "It's Clarence. It's Clarence."

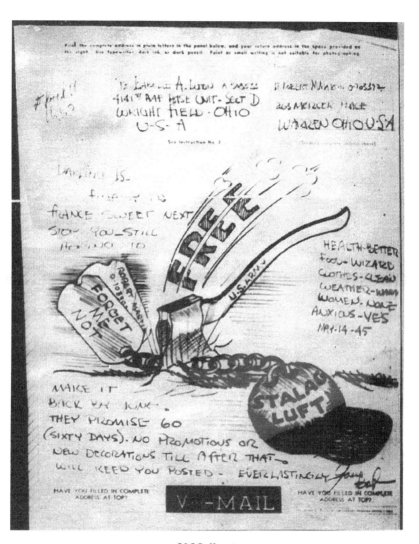

V-Mail art
Courtesy of Robert Martin (POW)

In the course of being in England, Ike and Churchill used a train to go out to see where the troops were. Our battalion was specified to supply the protection personnel for his train for a period of time and I was selected as one of the guards for the train. And so one night I am standing very stiffly at attention outside of a train door and Winnie steps out and he lights his cigar. So I had a few words of conversation with Mr. Churchill.

Norman P. Swaney
U.S. Army

Norm Swaney was drafted into the Army in January of 1942. During basic training, he heard they were looking for volunteers to become paratroopers.

Oh hell, that was the 'Glory Outfit.' You read all about them. I worked with two other guys and all three of us were going to join the paratroopers. The other two chickened out.

But not Norm; he volunteered and joined the 101st Airborne Division, 502nd Regiment, F Company. They trained for more than a year before they shipped out in the fall of 1943. Their ship ran into a little trouble on their Atlantic crossing.

*We were out west of Newfoundland someplace and a Gerry sub picked us up and these two little corvettes were cutting circles around us, dropping depth charges. And I don't know what it was, but all of a sudden there was an explosion on our ship. We were never told – did they race the engines too much and blow a boiler or were we hit. We don't know. But anyhow, the ship was watertight enough that we were able to get into St. Johns, Newfoundland. And we sat on the ship. Immediately, there was repair work of all sorts on the ship and eventually, they decided that we were going to go again. So we started out. They ran the ship aground. Back over to the harbor to do some more repair work and they finally decided **that** ship isn't going to make it. So we took the ship and instead of going overseas we went from St. Johns, Newfoundland to Halifax, Nova Scotia. They pulled us in there and immediately we transferred to another ship and headed for England. So we were forty-four days from the time we left New York till we got to England.*

The 101st finally arrived in Great Britain and began training for the invasion of France.

And we went into Liverpool and got into trains and went down to a camp about fifty miles outside of London, I guess. We trained for the next several months and a couple of times we practiced and assembled at the airport just for training purposes.

One day they were taken to an airfield and Norm thought this was it.

And then they decided D-Day was going to be a certain day. So the planes were there and we were loaded in and it didn't happen. Eisenhower or somebody decided it wouldn't happen.

The paratroopers returned to their camp and they waited. On June 4, 1944, they were again taken to the airfield; but once again, the invasion was delayed.

We never left the airport then. We stayed there that day.

On the evening of June 5ᵗʰ, General Eisenhower visited the 101ˢᵗ Airborne Division.

We were on the airfield on the 5ᵗʰ and then Ike came around and I talked to him and shook hands with him.

When Norm climbed on board a C-47 later that evening, he was ready.

I thought this is what we're here for. We're going to do it. It was a 'gung ho' situation. We're going in there and just tear things up. After all, we were convinced that we were the best in the world and I think we were.

Late that night, they parachuted into France. D-Day had begun.

The jump into Normandy was very, very peaceful for me. We were not where we were supposed to be, but I came down with virtually no firing right close to me. I could see it off in the distance. You could see tracers and stuff flying up and we could hear a lot of it before we jumped. But I came down and landed in a field and quickly stowed my chute out of the way because they were white and they showed up very well. I got my gun and everything and I didn't hear a sound and it was time for me to move. We had those little clicker things and I squeezed that a couple of times. No sound – nobody. So I decided well, I'm in the wrong field. It was a fairly small field with the big stone hedgerows and by laying down on the ground, and looking around, I could see that there was a gate. And so I slowly got over to the gate and went through the gate and squeezed the clicker again. Here's one of the guys right by the gate – one of my buddies. He said he was afraid to do the clicker. He was afraid to answer my clicker.

Company F was scattered around the French countryside.

It was pitch black, but in the course of, I suppose, the next hour, we gathered up nearly every one that jumped in the plane that I was in. But we came across a lieutenant who I had never seen before. Now where he came from, I don't know. But immediately the lieutenant took over control of the group. He had a map, so he could tell us where we were going, at least he said so. We had landed fairly close to the city or village of Carentan, which was nine miles from where we were supposed to be.

Their only option was to fight their way to their objective.

It took us two days, but eventually we got back with the company. They had already made the objective and got it out of the way. But in the course of going in those two days, we did a whole raft of skirmishes. For instance, we were going up a roadway with these darn hedgerows on both sides and came to one with a gate. And so you stopped and you made a run across because there might be somebody in that field. And we all made the run across there and one of my best buddies, who was the last man, decided there's nobody in that field and he just walked across and they shot him. That was the first guy I seen die, was him. He wouldn't run across. He must have thought, 'Hell, I don't have to run across. There's nobody there.' And so he got shot dead.

On a battlefield, you take cover wherever you can find it.

All of a sudden, I came across a dead cow. And you saw lots of animals – dead animals. This cow was laying off in the field and we were stopped in a line of skirmish there and that cow made the perfect cover for me. I laid my gun down behind that. The barrel fit right over the top of it. And that cow took an awful lot of beating, but it worked for me.

When there was a lull in the fighting, the men were ordered to look for prisoners and casualties.

We went out to gather up German prisoners or anybody, you know. And I was surprised at how many Germans we had killed there and how many were still laying there wounded. They were laying there overnight wounded and couldn't move. What can you do for them? Our medics were not mobile at that time. We didn't have ambulances or anything.

In six weeks of fighting in France, Norm's outfit suffered 30 percent casualties.

We were in Normandy from June 6th until late July and I never got a scratch. Yes, I got grazed three different times with shells, but not bad enough to be bothered with.

The 101st returned to Britain and waited for their next assignment.

We went back to England to recoup and rest up so that we could make another jump. And we prepared two or three times to jump, but didn't have to because the armored divisions were moving up faster than we expected.

Then the Allies came up with a bold plan that they thought would shorten the war. In September of 1944, the 101st took part in 'Operation Market Garden' – the invasion of Holland.

We were jumping in daylight and this was surprising. You could see the enormous volume of airplanes. And I was right at the open door of the plane and looking at it from where I was I saw one of the planes get hit and hit the ground. The engine went on fire and the plane went right down and hit the ground. But when we got to the landing area where we were going, there was nobody there. Hell, we landed on the ground and walked around like we were in Youngstown.

Swaney was a machine gunner. He needed a lot of ammunition to do his job and he relied on his squad to help out.

Machine guns use a lot and you had a squad of guys – a machine gunner, an assistant gunner, who carried a rifle and a tripod, and every other guy in the squad is supposed to have a box of ammunition for the machine gunner. We went racing across a field in one instance and came up to a road. The Germans were right on the opposite side of it. My assistant threw the tripod down; I set the gun up on it and looked around for ammunition. I didn't have any. I had to run back across this field and pick up two boxes of ammunition and come back and load the damn gun. I don't blame the guys, you know. If you're running across the field to beat hell and you've got a rifle in one hand and a box of ammunition in the other hand – and you're supposed to hit the ground every so often just so you don't get shot – pretty soon that box of ammunition is useless. And so they dropped them.

And the soldier with the machine gun was a prime target for the enemy.

I set up my machine gun and laid out a hell of a field of fire for a while. And the Germans realized where I was at and they cut the trees down around me with heavy weapons. So I got loaded with shrapnel and that was my end for being in Holland.

Norm was seriously wounded by the shrapnel.

I was pulled out of the line. The medic took a look at me and ripped my shirt open and said, "We're going to evacuate you." And so a jeep came along and they loaded me on the jeep. I'm still walking, no problem. We go back to an aid station someplace and the doc looked at me and they peeled my shirt up from behind and I was full of shrapnel in the back. I didn't know how bad I was. I knew I had lost a lot of blood. So they put me in a British ambulance and we started off for someplace. And the next thing I remember is being in a hospital in England. I woke up and I was in a big tub, soaking in hot water, trying to get the shrapnel pieces out.

In December of 1944, Swaney rejoined the 101st Airborne Division in France. He had only been away for a couple of months, but there were a lot of new faces in his outfit.

I didn't know half the guys. My one buddy, who had been my assistant machine gunner at one time, was now my sergeant. And one of the guys, who I never thought would be up for promotion, was the top sergeant of the whole company. And so things were quite changed and the guys that I was with – I didn't know a one of them. They were brand new people to me.

In mid-December, the Battle of the Bulge began and the 101st was back in action.

Our battalion was sent to a position north of the Bastogne village, itself. We went in trucks and got in so close and then got out and walked. And I mean, we traveled and traveled and traveled, trying to get to where we were supposed to be. Then we moved a couple of times and finally they decided we're going to hold this perimeter. And that was fine. We had no trouble holding the perimeter at all. In fact, we had little activity, not much at all. Occasionally, you'd see a German off in the distance and you'd lay a couple of rounds towards him and he'd disappear and that was the end of that. You wouldn't see any more for a while. But it was colder than Hell.

Every veteran of The Battle of the Bulge remembers the bitter cold.

And I mean it was so cold that you had one heck of a time chopping that out to get a foxhole dug. And then you get something to cover it so you could stay under cover and keep an eye out to see where things were. And you were trying to stay warm down in the ground. The company decided that a few guys at a time needed to get back and cleaned and rested. Our boots were filthy and our overcoats were muddy and everything. So I was pulled off the line – my buddy and I, both of us – and we went back to a house. Great. We had a full night's sleep in a warm house. Boy, what a relief that was. And in the morning, I got up. My good jump boots were all covered with mud and dirt and the first thing I did was clean them up and set them out. And the sun was shining. I did the same with my overcoat. I cleaned it and hung it outside. And the word came that there's a tank attack coming. I don't have a gun. So we're going to the front line and there's a lieutenant and he handed me a radio. He says, "You're my radio operator." And I still don't have a weapon. We get up on the front line and fortunately, we were able to get into a swale and truthfully, I don't know why the lieutenant didn't seem to have any direction for anybody. He didn't say anything to anybody. He didn't do anything. We just stayed there and he never asked for the radio or anything. And I don't suppose we'd been up on the front line more than fifteen minutes when there was a German behind me. He says, "Roust! Roust!" And that was it. We had been watching a tank coming at us and the tank got up so close and stopped. Apparently, the tank commander knew that the Germans were coming around. The Germans were all behind us before we even knew it. So that's when we were taken prisoner.

Norm and more than forty soldiers were captured.

We went back the first night and the whole group of us were put into a barn. There were some bleeding, some not bleeding, and some of us in pretty good shape, some not. We were interrogated by an officer, individually and collectively, and I don't think he found anything out of any importance because none of us knew what in the hell was going on anyhow.

The prisoners who were in good shape were immediately put to work.

They had a whole raft of German women and older men, the home guard and so on, felling trees; and doing this all by hand – all with axes and so on. And we as prisoners were the guys that gathered up all the branches and stacked them up and eventually, those were all used. There was never a trace of wood left. It was gone someplace.

I worked there for probably a week and then, moved on again, this time into Limburg. Limburg, Germany is a railroad area. Our job there was to repair the railroad. They'd take a whole group of us out at night. Some of us were given a shovel and we filled holes where it had been bombed and we moved rails and all sorts of things that you would do for the railroad. By daylight, you were back in a compound and the British would come over and bomb it out again.

More prisoners of war arrived in Limburg and Swaney's group was moved deeper into Germany.

I came to another compound. I didn't know what the situation was, but a German came in and he spoke English. He was looking for farmers.

"Yeah, I was a farmer."

"Do you know how to drive a horse?"

"Yes, I know how to drive a horse."

So for a number of days, I was a horseman at an airport. I had one horse and during the course of the day, I took care of the horse. If they wanted the horse to pull a little cart, the German guard would say to go here and there. Maybe we'd pick up a piece for an airplane on this little cart. Then you'd change the hitch and use the horse to pull an engine up so they can put it in an airplane. Everything was done manually. There was no mobile equipment. Just that horse of mine. And I thoroughly enjoyed it. Hell, being a prisoner wasn't too bad. I had a horse and a half-warm place to sleep and I wasn't starved. So I thoroughly enjoyed that.

Norm's experiences as a prisoner of war were certainly not typical.

Well, that horseman job didn't last a whole lot of time. I was moved on back to another area and I was in a German mobile bakery – a military bakery. The vehicles would come in at night with the sawdust and the flour and whatever was needed and we would unload it and do other chores around there. I must have been in that place for maybe three weeks. I don't know how long I was there. But that wasn't too bad either. At least I was fairly warm during the night and we had some days that were half-decent.

After spending nearly three months on various labor details, Swaney boarded a train bound for a prison camp.

We were packed in tight enough that we slept on each other. You had no other choice. One corner was used as a urinal and that's about all you had – was a urinal – because nobody ever had to take a…because you didn't have any food. The one thing I will say, it was warm because there were so many of us. But by this time, we had all developed a series of bedbugs and lice, so when it got warm, you got itchy.

A few weeks after they arrived at the camp, reports came in that elements of Patton's 3rd Army were approaching. The camp Kommandant assembled the prisoners and made an announcement.

And he said that you guys can do what you want. "We're going to lock the gates and we're going to leave. If you try to escape, you'll probably be shot." He said, "If you stay here, you'll live and your American troops will soon be here."

We had three guys that escaped. They got out of the fence and they got back in too, later on.

The camp was liberated and Norm Swaney was headed home. When he got back to the States, his family was very surprised to learn where he had been.

I called from New York. They were shocked that I was there. My mother told me they never got a telex. And I have the telex of when I was wounded, but they never got a telex to the effect that I had been taken prisoner.

When you're only about nineteen years old and you're living a kind of a laid-back lifestyle like that and then, all of a sudden in the matter of less than an hour almost, this whole chaotic thing happened and the whole, damn world turned upside down. And the loss of all your buddies and that. Well, it sure matured you in a hell of a hurry. I'll say that. You got a little maturity out of that.

Dick Becker
U.S. Navy

During his senior year in high school, Dick Becker was facing an uncertain future. He decided to join the Navy.

That was in '39. I had nothing better to do. I had no prospect of going to school. My father couldn't afford college or anything. Work was scarce. So, it seemed the logical thing to do.

After boot camp, Becker was assigned to the supply ship *Antares*. He was one of the ship's firemen. He worked below deck with a group of sailors nicknamed 'the Black Gang.'

We in the Black Gang, or the firemen, fired the boilers. This old ship was a World War One ship, which had been converted from a coal-burner to oil, so we didn't have to shovel coal. But it was a natural draft ship. They hadn't incorporated pressurized fire rooms and it was a hot son of a gun down there with them boilers.

Since the *Antares* was a supply ship, she had no guns.

The supply, repair, oilers and all that, were called the base force. So we were a member of the base force and at that time, the secondary ships were going to be protected in a task force or a task group by the armed ships and the fighting ships. So there were no guns on there. We had no armament to defend ourselves. Supposedly, someone else was going to protect us.

In the months before America entered World War Two, the country was preparing for the inevitable.

They were in the process of developing the forward islands in anticipation of potential engagement with Japan. That was on the burner already, way back then.

One of the jobs for the *Antares* was transporting equipment and supplies to these islands.

The ship would go from Pearl Harbor, which we really considered our home port because we so seldom came back to the States. We would take on a load of cargo, men, equipment, or whatever, and go out to Johnson Island, Palmira Island, Midway,

Wake, Phoenix Islands – just all over, and pretty lengthy cruises.

Some of the islands were not much more than a rock in the ocean.

We went out into a lot of these forward areas before there was anything established there. Johnson Island later on became one of the key air landing strips and it was a volcanic peak when we got there. This one little chunk was sticking out of the ocean and everybody said what the hell are they going to do here? An airplane can't land by dropping down on that sucker. But they whittled off the top and pushed it both ways and elongated it and made an airstrip there. The same was literally true of Midway Islands. They were just little atolls, but they got a strip on there.

Dick wanted to be a pilot. When the *Antares* returned to Pearl Harbor, he spent his pay on flying lessons. Some of the other sailors had other ideas.

Most of the guys would head for shore and find themselves the prostitutes and the bars and that scene and I didn't want that. I was so determined with this flying and that's pretty expensive. You've got to remember enlisted men, at that time frame, got twenty-one bucks a month. That doesn't go very far – seventy-five cents a day.

In October of 1941, the *Antares* was sent to the Phoenix Islands.

The Phoenix Islands were a British possession. They are out in the south Pacific, below the equator, and the British had agreed to allow the Americans to come in and build a runway. The only thing that was operating there was a seaplane tender station. It was a stop en route for refueling for the Pan Am China Clipper. We would not only load the ship up, but we would tow barges behind and we took the men and the heavy equipment to begin constructing the runway up there.

After nearly two months, they returned to Pearl Harbor.

We left in October and didn't come back until December the 7th. We arrived that morning. They had the submarine net across the mouth of the harbor to prevent somebody sneaking in. They wouldn't open that until daylight. We arrived there early in the morning and it was still dark, so the ship just circled right in the mouth of the harbor.

Becker woke up early on the morning of December 7, 1941.

I had the upcoming eight to twelve watch. We used to stand watches, as they called them, either four on and four off or eight on and eight off. And I had to come up early to eat breakfast and then go down and relieve the guys who were down there, so they could come up for breakfast and complete their watch. So I was up like at six o'clock that morning and we were up topside, waiting for them to pipe down chow to let you know you can come in and eat. In fact, my one buddy, Harry Ryan, was standing there on the deck and we were both looking at this damn submarine coming toward us, like the guy's going to ram us. It didn't look big enough to be a real submarine and we wondered, 'What the hell is going on?' The next thing we knew, we saw the Ward. She was the picket destroyer out there. Our ship had called them for assistance and they came around our bow and ka-blam! They shot that sucker right in the conning tower. That was the first shot fired in World War Two. And I was standing there watching that thing and didn't know what was going on, but had the ringside seat. Now that was at 6:30.

The attack of the midget submarines was the first phase of the surprise attack. Less than ninety minutes later, the main attack on Pearl Harbor began. The *Antares* cut loose the barge that they had been towing.

We had decided to chop loose the barge because we couldn't maneuver the ship very well with that tow. And at about that time, at 7:55 of course, the main attack started. And we chopped that cable and cast that thing adrift. They made strafing runs and attempted bombing runs, but being a secondary target, they didn't make the concerted effort that they did for the big ships.

The *Antares* was just a couple of miles from the entrance to Pearl Harbor during the attack.

Probably the largest explosion, even bigger than the Arizona, was a destroyer in the floating dry dock. I can't think of the name. Anyway, when they hit that sucker, the magazines blew and the flames must have went five- to eight-hundred feet in the air. So we knew things were pretty bad or suspected that things were pretty bad.

Dick heard that destroyer explode, but he didn't see it. When 'General Quarters' sounded, he had to report to his station.

In an emergency situation, they sound General Quarters. The klaxon goes off and sirens go off and you go to your appointed station. Mine happened to be the engine room and that's well below the water line and there're no windows down there to look out. And the concussion of the explosions feels like the bomb or the torpedo is coming through the side of the hull. You don't know what the hell is happening. And they tell you to constantly inspect the ship's plates to see if the rivets have popped and if it's leaking. You're down there in an environment, you know. If you were up topside and you would be breathing fresh air and seeing what's going on, you'd have some degree of security or something. But you're down there. And I can remember the engineering officer coming down there and strapping on his 45 and he stood at the top of these little ladders and catwalks that you go up to get out of there and he said, "I'm going to shoot the first man that comes up here." I tell you, you get into a little bit of a panic situation down there among that machinery and that. You hear these bombs exploding close to you and that impact on the hull. Jesus Christ, man, you know? That just wouldn't seem to be the place you'd want to be. They should let you get up topside, so if you're going to sink or something, you've got a Chinaman's chance to get off. I do remember that. And I've got to admit I was pretty damned concerned.

The attack continued and the *Antares* kept circling outside of Pearl Harbor.

Because we were underway and maneuvering the ship, we were a moving target and they didn't do so good with us. All the ships in the harbor were tied up and just sitting ducks. So we survived everything and nobody got hit, shot or hurt.

Late in the day, the skipper of the *Antares* was told he could head into port.

They told us not to come in and block the channel, so we went into Honolulu Harbor. And then later that evening, we came back into Pearl Harbor and God, when you sailed in there, oh wow, all the oil on the water and things burning and the bodies. Man, what a mess. It was a very sobering situation. Then that night, the assumption was that the Japs are going to take over this place. They're going to bring landing forces. They had devastated it so they knew that there would be little or no resistance. I don't think they knew how well off they had it. If they had brought some landing forces, I think they could have taken those islands and held them without a hell of a lot of trouble.

Becker had guard duty that night.

I was given a watch out on the dock and they said to challenge and don't hesitate if you don't get the password. And where we used to tie up, across from 10-10 docks, there were some warehouses. I remember firing off a few rounds at – I don't know if it was a cat or what the hell it was – but jeez, I wasn't going to wait for somebody. If they didn't give me some recognition signal in a hell of a hurry, shoot.

And I shot and then that would draw fire from somebody else and pretty soon, you're shooting at each other. Stupid as could be.

Much later, Becker remembered that he missed an appointment on December 7th.

I was scheduled to fly the morning of the 7th at what is the John Rogers Airport in Honolulu.

If the *Antares* had arrived just a little earlier, he could have found himself in the middle of the action in the air.

In the movie Tora! Tora! Tora! in the scenes as they begin the bombing, they show a little yellow airplane with a female instructor and a student. She's caught in between all these Japanese coming in. I could have very well been in that airplane had I gotten ashore because I had time scheduled. I would have been out there flying.

Salvage operations began almost immediately at Pearl Harbor and the *Antares* helped with the recovery.

About the only thing they didn't recover was the old Utah. It was a battleship that was used as a target ship and it was not a part of the first line Navy. And of course, they didn't salvage the Arizona because that whole hull was just a mess. The West Virginia was sunk. The California was sunk. The Nevada was beached and sunk, the Ogalala ... I'm trying to remember all of them – oh the Shaw, that's the one I was trying to remember from before. The destroyer Shaw was in the floating dry-dock and the bomb that blew the forward magazine and everything cut that ship right in half, sank the dry-dock and the whole works. The back end of this ship was almost intact and they were already building the front end of the ship back in Mare Island Navy Yard. It looked like somebody took a big hatchet and chopped this sucker in half. They welded these temporary plates and got it floated and brought it alongside our ship. The reason they brought it to us was because we had a King Boom, which could lift an extremely heavy load. They had prefabricated a little v-bow to put on to the front section of the Shaw and they were going to sail it back to the States. They built a little tiny bridge up there for somebody to steer and see. And we hoisted that bow section out and held it in place while they welded it on. That salvage operation in itself had to be a marvelous engineering feat to save what they saved of all of those ships that were sunk, laying on their sides and, jeez.

Dick had submitted numerous requests for a transfer to flight school. In the spring of 1942, his request was approved.

In April, my orders came and it said for me to leave the ship and wait for transportation back to the States to enroll in the program commencing on the 26ᵗʰ of May (1942). I think I was almost a month in the receiving ship.

While he waited, he continued to work with a salvage crew.

Yeah, I was working on the ships. I worked on the West Virginia, raising her. I worked on the California. We were still burying bodies and that was a mess.

Becker became an enlisted Naval Aviation Pilot – a 'White Hat.' For the remainder of the war, he flew non-combat missions to just about every corner of the Pacific. After V-J Day, he flew over Japan.

We flew out of Okinawa and we went up into Japan as occupational forces. We flew around there taking a look at the destruction of the bombings, particularly Hiroshima and Nagasaki. And that's a very sobering thing to see. What were these huge communities – just a skeletal mess. And one bomb did this. And we've made eons of progress in the few short years since that time. So the next time around, if it really becomes a world conflagration, I don't know what the hell to expect. I won't be here probably, but I hope you guys can handle it.

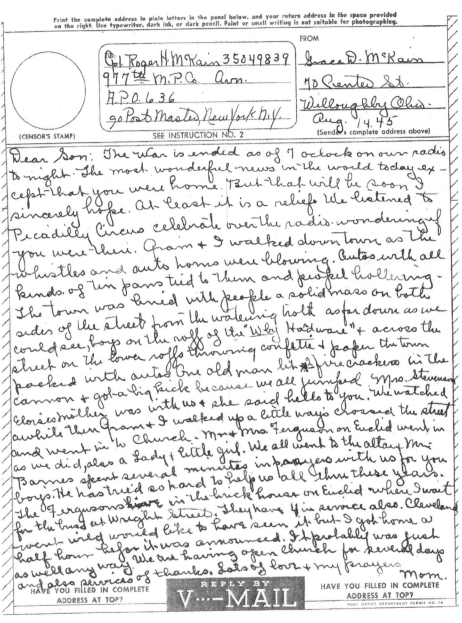

FROM

Cpl. Roger H McKain 35049839
977th M.P.Co. Avn.
A.P.O. 636
go Post Master, New York N.Y.

Grace D. McKain
70 Renter St.
Willoughby Ohio.
Aug. 14.45
(Sender's complete address above)

(CENSOR'S STAMP)   SEE INSTRUCTION NO. 2

Dear Son: The War is ended as of 7 oclock on our radio to night. The most wonderful news in the world today except that you were home. But that will be soon I sincerely hope. At least it is a relief. We listened to Picadilly Circus celebrate over the radio. wondering if you were there. Gram & I walked down town as the whistles and auto horns were blowing. Autos with all kinds of tin pans tied to them and people hollering. The town was lined with people a solid mass on both sides of the street from the watering trolk as far down as we could see, boys on the roff of the "Why Hardware" & across the street on the lower roffs throwing confetti & paper the town packed with autos One old man lit fire crackers in the cannon & got a big kick because we all jumped Mrs. Stevens Eloise's mother was with us & she said hello to you. We watched awhile then Gram & I walked up a little ways crossed the street and went in to Church. Mr & Mrs. Ferguson on Euclid went in as we did, also a Lady & little girl. We all went to the altar Mr. Barnes spent several minutes in prayers with us for you boys. He has tried so hard to help us all thru these years. The Fergusons live in the brick house on Euclid where I wait for the bus at Wright Street. They have 4 in service also. Cleveland went wild would like to have seen it but I got home a half hour before it was announced. It probably was just as well any way. We are having open church for several days and also services of thanks. Lots of love & my prayers
Mom.

Courtesy of Roger McKain

When Tom Kopke read I was working with The Veterans History Project, he wanted to share his story with me and it didn't matter to him that it would be a little out of his way. He drove from his home in Dearborn, Michigan to Cleveland to do an interview.

Tom was drafted in 1943. He was hoping to join the Army Air Force, but he bumped his head on a bus door on the way to the induction center. When he took his physical, he was just a little too tall for the Air Force – in fact, a bump on the head too tall. Kopke was assigned to the 88th Infantry Division and served in Italy.

Tom recorded the following story for the LEGACIES radio series. This is his original essay of his most vivid memory of the war.

Thomas L. Kopke
U.S. Army
EASTER SUNDAY – 1944

Of the 1,348 days that the United States was engaged in World War II, there are many that have a significant meaning to me. However, there is one, more than all the others, that is indelibly etched in my mind. That day is April 9, 1944.

On that day, Company E, of the 88th Infantry Division's 349th Regiment, was dug in on the forward slope of a mountain, west of Casino, Italy. The 88th Infantry Division was the first all-draftee division committed to action in World War II. Until that time all of our troops fighting around the world were either units of the Regular Army or the National Guard. Because no one knew what to expect from this group of draftees, the Division was assigned to a quiet zone on the Italian Front. The Anzio Beachhead was 65 miles to the north, just south of Rome. Operation Overlord, the Normandy invasion, was still two months away. Yes, this was the time of the quiet war. The cold rains of the Italian winter turned what soil there was into slick mud, not conducive to large-scale troop movements. There were nightly patrols by both sides to try to find weak spots along the line that might be exploited once spring arrived.

When I said we were "dug in," it was a misnomer; since the rocky mountainside precluded digging a normal foxhole. Rock after rock was piled one on top of another in a circle large enough to provide above ground protection for usually three soldiers. Across a small valley was the enemy. German infantrymen occupied more permanent protection in their vaunted Gustav Line on Mount Damiano. We had been on line for approximately two weeks. Two weeks without a change of clothes, except for the extra pair of socks that most of us carried. It would be another two weeks before we would be relieved and could visit a delousing center to take a shower and be refitted with a new set of clothes.

Our food consisted of either "C" or "K" rations, depending upon which were delivered by mule train each night. Since lighting a fire was not permitted, it was necessary to eat the food cold as it came from the can. It was easy to lose track of exactly what day it was since the mule train did not deliver copies of the "Stars and Stripes" newspaper and personal transistor radios were unknown. There was no mail delivery, so for a month at a time we did not receive or send mail. Days were spent trying to sleep. Raising your head above the rim of the rocks invited sniper fire. On nights when you were not on patrol, two of the three in each hole had to remain alert to constantly watch or listen for possible movement of the enemy in front of you. This was the life of the average front line GI on a good day. You try not to remember the bad days. It is easy to realize why foot soldiers throughout the ages adopted the philosophy of "Eat, Drink, and Make Merry, For Tomorrow You may Be Dead."

A little before dawn on Sunday, April 9, 1944, the word was passed from hole to hole that we were to withhold any rifle fire until further notice. No reason was given, but several times in the past similar orders had been received. On those occasions, medical corpsmen, under Red Cross flags, ventured into no man's land to retrieve the body of a fallen comrade, a casualty on one of the patrols. Both the Americans and Germans performed and observed these acts of wartime courtesy. Along with the two other GIs in my hole, I believed that this would again be the case.

No doubt similar orders were passed along the fortified Gustav Line. About a half-hour later, a second message was received, "It's Easter Sunday." The question on almost everyone's mind was what Easter Sunday had to do with our withholding fire. An hour or so later we were to find out. Instead of medics, we observed soldiers from the Division Quartermaster Company. They wove their way through the minefields, along a path cleared by the Engineers. It was marked with white rags on short sticks. Instead of a body, they carried various-size boxes on a litter. We observed them stop near the center of the valley and begin to assemble a public address system. Once the sun had risen above the mountains to our East, we observed the two Chaplains attached to the Division make their way along the same path. Over the public address system, Catholic Chaplain Leo Crowley conducted an abridged Mass in Latin. He was followed by Chaplain Oscar Reinboth, a Lutheran minister, who delivered in both English and German, the glorious Easter message of Christ's resurrection.

Surely, this message was meant just for us. Were we not fighting for the Four Freedoms spelled out by President Franklin D. Roosevelt? He described these as the worldwide goals of the United States foreign policy. Namely, the freedom of speech and religion, as well as, the freedom from want and fear. With such lofty goals, God had to be on our side. What possible reason could there be for God to side with the Germans?

Yet the belt buckles of several Germans we had captured on patrol carried the message – "Gott Mit Uns," which translated means "God With Us." It was on Easter Sunday morning, on a mountainside in Italy, that I reaffirmed the religious belief of my childhood. For I finally realized that God had sent His beloved Son, Jesus, to all peoples of the world and whoever believed in Him would share in that glorious message "He is not here; for he has been raised, even as he has said."

The chaplains returned from no man's land, the Quartermaster personnel dismantled the public address system. Even before the sun reached the midpoint of its journey across the sky, the order came down to resume firing. For a few short hours on Sunday, April 9, 1944, there was Peace on Earth and Goodwill among men, even if it occurred on only one small segment of a war-weary world.

It would be another thirteen months before V-E Day ended the conflict in Europe. So many times during the intervening fifty-nine years I have wondered, why the peace that prevailed for those few hours on Easter Sunday, could not have been expanded to save thousands of lives. Could we have avoided Omaha Beach, Hiroshima, and Nagasaki? Would it have been possible to avoid the division of Europe that resulted in the Cold War? How much different the last half of the Twentieth Century would have been if only everyone in the world could have believed – "Gott Mit Uns."

AFTER IT'S OVER

"After it's over, over here,
I'll come home to you, dear,
You've been blue,
But oh, so true,
Now this is what we'll do,
We'll build a little place with a garden,
Just a little home for two,
And we'll be so happy there,
We'll live without a care,
Making our dreams come true, together"

~ C. Swope & C. Rippey

LEGACIES:

Stories from the Second World War

– The Radio Series –

Hear the voices of history:

More than 165 shows have been produced for the **LEGACIES** radio series and they are now available on CD. Each week a guest shares personal memories of World War Two. You will hear compelling stories told by the men and women who were there. Guests include veterans of Pearl Harbor, D-Day, The Battle of the Bulge, Iwo Jima and Okinawa; survivors of The Blitz and The Bataan Death March, and many more. These half-hour programs are individual portraits of the human drama of war. Many veterans are telling the stories of their lives during the war for the first time. **LEGACIES** also includes original music from the war years.

<u>LEGACIES: *Stories from the Second World War*</u>

– **Ohio Excellence in Journalism Award:**
  Press Club of Cleveland / Human-interest category – 2007.

– **Best Weekly Show in Northeast Ohio:**
  The March of Dimes / A.I.R. (Achievement in Radio) Award – 2002.

– **Ohio Excellence in Journalism Award:**
  Press Club of Cleveland / Human-interest category – 2002.

Each CD includes two shows. For a complete catalog, contact:

Tom Swope
Producer and Narrator of **LEGACIES: *Stories from the Second World War***
(440) 255-7410

e-mail: swopetunes@juno.com

The Veterans History Project

The Veterans History Project is a nationwide volunteer effort of the American Folklife Center at the Library of Congress, to record and preserve the stories of wartime veterans and civilian war workers. The effort relies on thousands of volunteers across the country who interview veterans of all wars, as well as those who supported them on the home front.

Those interested in becoming involved in the Veterans History Project are encouraged to e-mail vohp@loc.gov to request a project kit. The kit is also available on the VHP website – www.loc.gov/vets – or by calling the toll-free message line at (888) 371-5848.

Made in the USA
Charleston, SC
27 August 2011